B E

Identification Record Book

Hello Wild

Your Feedback is Appreciated!!!

Please consider leaving us "5 Stars" on your
Amazon review.

Thank you!

This Bee Identification Record Book
Belongs To:

_____

Location / GPS: _____ Date _____

Habitat: ◯ Garden ◯ Forest ◯ Woodland ◯ Orchard ◯ Meadow
◯ Other _____

Nest: ◯ Hive ◯ Wood ◯ Tree ◯ Hollow Stem/Reed ◯ Crevice/Edge
◯ Other _____

Climate Type: ◯ Dry ◯ Temperate ◯ Tropical ◯ Other _____

Weather Conditions _____

Color: ◯ Black ◯ Yellow ◯ Brown ◯ White ◯ Blue ◯ Red
◯ Orange ◯ Purple ◯ Green ◯ Striped ◯ (Other) _____

Body: ◯ Round/Chubby ◯ Slender ◯ Furry ◯ (Other) _____

Stinger: ◯ Yes ◯ No

Behavior: ◯ Solitary ◯ Brood ◯ Social ◯ Parasitic ◯ Aggressive
◯ (Other) _____

Notes: _____

Wings
Head
Antennae
Thorax
Foreleg
Middle Leg
Hindleg
Thorax

Sketch

a.
Similar to drone but have space between eyes.

b.
Similar to worker but have shorter proboscis.

c.
Have huge eyes that touch top of head.

a. Worker / b. Queen / c. Drone
◯ ◯ ◯

Only female bees have stingers.

♀ All worker bees are female.

○ Worker

Pollen basket

Drone bees are the only male bees in the hive. ♂

○ Drone

○ Queen

♀ Only bee capable of laying fertilized eggs.

No stingers.

Huge eyes that meet at the top of the head.

No hairs. Exoskeleton is smooth and brightly colored.

Shorty, stubby antennae.

Two pairs of wings (often folded together similar to bees).

Only one pair of wings.

Fly

Very pinched waist (between thorax and abdomen) and long narrow body.

Wasp

Behavior to look for:
Flies hover very steadily. Bees do not hover.

Behavior to look for:
May take time collecting flower nectar vs bees which tend to move deliberately and quickly.

Location / GPS: _____ Date _____

Habitat: ◯ Garden ◯ Forest ◯ Woodland ◯ Orchard ◯ Meadow
◯ Other _____

Nest: ◯ Hive ◯ Wood ◯ Tree ◯ Hollow Stem/Reed ◯ Crevice/Edge
◯ Other _____

Climate Type: ◯ Dry ◯ Temperate ◯ Tropical ◯ Other_____

Weather Conditions _____

Color: ◯ Black ◯ Yellow ◯ Brown ◯ White ◯ Blue ◯ Red
◯ Orange ◯ Purple ◯ Green ◯ Striped ◯(Other) _____

Body: ◯ Round/Chubby ◯ Slender ◯ Furry ◯(Other) _____

Stinger: ◯ Yes ◯ No

Behavior: ◯ Solitary ◯ Brood ◯ Social ◯ Parasitic ◯ Aggressive
◯(Other) _____

Notes: _____

- Wings
- Head
- Antennae
- Thorax
- Foreleg
- Middle Leg
- Hindleg
- Thorax

Sketch

a. Similar to drone but have space between eyes.

b. Similar to worker but have shorter proboscis.

c. Have huge eyes that touch top of head.

a. <u>Worker</u> / b. <u>Queen</u> / c. <u>Drone</u>
◯ ◯ ◯

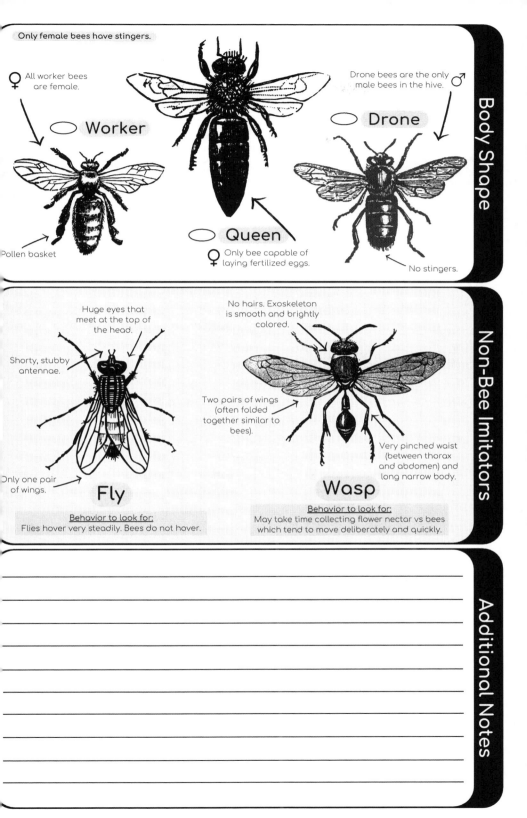

Only female bees have stingers.

♀ All worker bees are female.

Worker

♂ Drone bees are the only male bees in the hive.

Drone

Queen

♀ Only bee capable of laying fertilized eggs.

Pollen basket

No stingers.

Huge eyes that meet at the top of the head.

Shorty, stubby antennae.

No hairs. Exoskeleton is smooth and brightly colored.

Two pairs of wings (often folded together similar to bees).

Very pinched waist (between thorax and abdomen) and long narrow body.

Only one pair of wings.

Fly

Wasp

Behavior to look for:
Flies hover very steadily. Bees do not hover.

Behavior to look for:
May take time collecting flower nectar vs bees which tend to move deliberately and quickly.

Location / GPS: _____ Date _____

Habitat: ◯ Garden ◯ Forest ◯ Woodland ◯ Orchard ◯ Meadow
◯ Other _____

Nest: ◯ Hive ◯ Wood ◯ Tree ◯ Hollow Stem/Reed ◯ Crevice/Edge
◯ Other _____

Climate Type: ◯ Dry ◯ Temperate ◯ Tropical ◯ Other_____

Weather Conditions _____

Color: ◯ Black ◯ Yellow ◯ Brown ◯ White ◯ Blue ◯ Red
◯ Orange ◯ Purple ◯ Green ◯ Striped ◯ (Other) _____

Body: ◯ Round/Chubby ◯ Slender ◯ Furry ◯ (Other) _____

Stinger: ◯ Yes ◯ No

Behavior: ◯ Solitary ◯ Brood ◯ Social ◯ Parasitic ◯ Aggressive
◯ (Other) _____

Notes: _____

Wings → Head

Antennae

Thorax

Foreleg

Middle Leg

Thorax →

Hindleg

Sketch

a. Similar to drone but have space between eyes.

b. Similar to worker but have shorter proboscis.

c. Have huge eyes that touch top of head.

a. **Worker** / b. **Queen** / c. **Drone**
◯ ◯ ◯

Only female bees have stingers.

♀ All worker bees are female.

◯ Worker

Drone bees are the only male bees in the hive. ♂

◯ Drone

◯ Queen

♀ Only bee capable of laying fertilized eggs.

Pollen basket

No stingers.

Huge eyes that meet at the top of the head.

No hairs. Exoskeleton is smooth and brightly colored.

Shorty, stubby antennae.

Two pairs of wings (often folded together similar to bees).

Only one pair of wings.

Fly

Very pinched waist (between thorax and abdomen) and long narrow body.

Wasp

Behavior to look for:
Flies hover very steadily. Bees do not hover.

Behavior to look for:
May take time collecting flower nectar vs bees which tend to move deliberately and quickly.

Location / GPS: _____ Date _____

Habitat: ◯ Garden ◯ Forest ◯ Woodland ◯ Orchard ◯ Meadow
◯ Other _____

Nest: ◯ Hive ◯ Wood ◯ Tree ◯ Hollow Stem/Reed ◯ Crevice/Edge
◯ Other _____

Climate Type: ◯ Dry ◯ Temperate ◯ Tropical ◯ Other_____

Weather Conditions _____

General

Color: ◯ Black ◯ Yellow ◯ Brown ◯ White ◯ Blue ◯ Red
◯ Orange ◯ Purple ◯ Green ◯ Striped ◯ (Other) _____

Body: ◯ Round/Chubby ◯ Slender ◯ Furry ◯ (Other) _____

Stinger: ◯ Yes ◯ No

Behavior: ◯ Solitary ◯ Brood ◯ Social ◯ Parasitic ◯ Aggressive
◯ (Other) _____

Notes: _____

Characteristics

Wings

Head

Antennae

Thorax

Thorax

Foreleg

Middle Leg

Hindleg

Sketch

Head Shape

a.
Similar to drone but have space between eyes.

b.
Similar to worker but have shorter proboscis.

c.
Have huge eyes that touch top of head.

a. **Worker** / b. **Queen** / c. **Drone**
◯   ◯   ◯

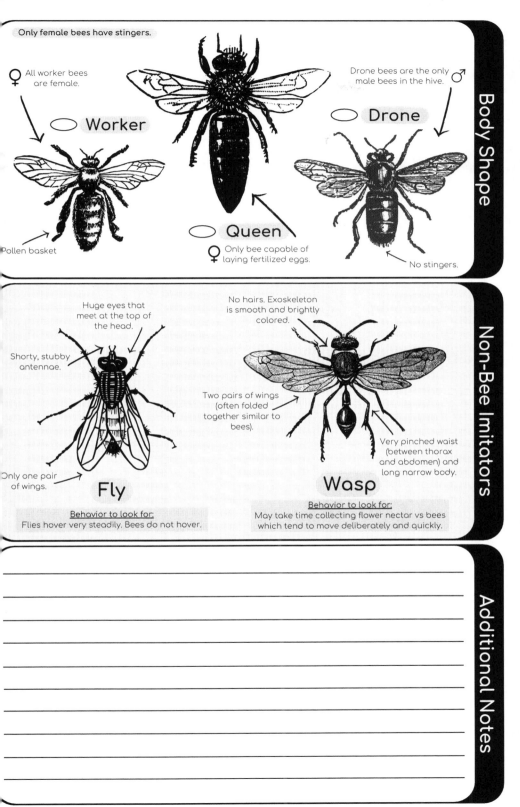

Only female bees have stingers.

♀ All worker bees are female.

Drone bees are the only male bees in the hive. ♂

Worker

Drone

Queen

♀ Only bee capable of laying fertilized eggs.

Pollen basket

No stingers.

Huge eyes that meet at the top of the head.

No hairs. Exoskeleton is smooth and brightly colored.

Shorty, stubby antennae.

Two pairs of wings (often folded together similar to bees).

Very pinched waist (between thorax and abdomen) and long narrow body.

Only one pair of wings.

Fly

Wasp

Behavior to look for:
Flies hover very steadily. Bees do not hover.

Behavior to look for:
May take time collecting flower nectar vs bees which tend to move deliberately and quickly.

Environment

Location / GPS: _____ Date _____

Habitat: ◯ Garden ◯ Forest ◯ Woodland ◯ Orchard ◯ Meadow
◯ Other _____

Nest: ◯ Hive ◯ Wood ◯ Tree ◯ Hollow Stem/Reed ◯ Crevice/Edge
◯ Other _____

Climate Type: ◯ Dry ◯ Temperate ◯ Tropical ◯ Other_____

Weather Conditions _____

General

Color: ◯ Black ◯ Yellow ◯ Brown ◯ White ◯ Blue ◯ Red
◯ Orange ◯ Purple ◯ Green ◯ Striped ◯ (Other) _____

Body: ◯ Round/Chubby ◯ Slender ◯ Furry ◯ (Other) _____

Stinger: ◯ Yes ◯ No

Behavior: ◯ Solitary ◯ Brood ◯ Social ◯ Parasitic ◯ Aggressive
◯ (Other) _____

Notes: _____

Characteristics

Wings
Head
Antennae
Thorax
Thorax
Foreleg
Middle Leg
Hindleg

Sketch

Head Shape

a. Similar to drone but have space between eyes.

b. Similar to worker but have shorter proboscis.

c. Have huge eyes that touch top of head.

a. **Worker** / b. **Queen** / c. **Drone**
◯ ◯ ◯

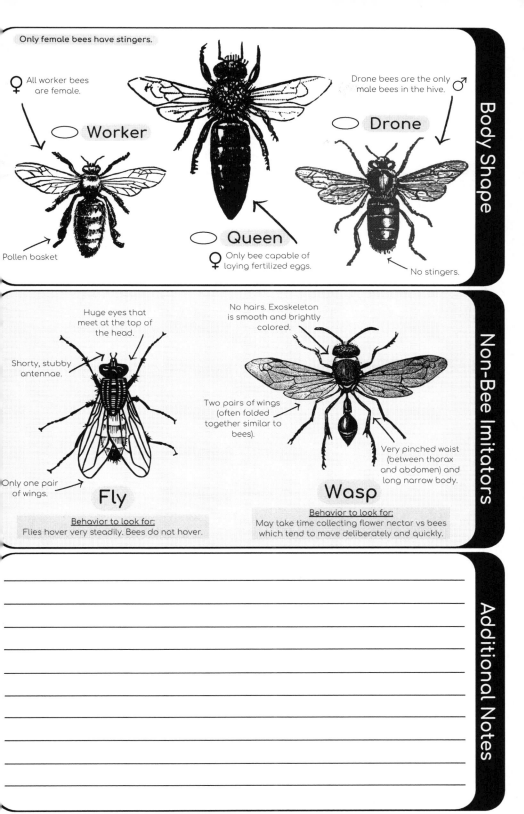

Only female bees have stingers.

All worker bees are female.

Worker

Drone bees are the only male bees in the hive.

Drone

Queen

Pollen basket

Only bee capable of laying fertilized eggs.

No stingers.

Huge eyes that meet at the top of the head.

No hairs. Exoskeleton is smooth and brightly colored.

Shorty, stubby antennae.

Two pairs of wings (often folded together similar to bees).

Only one pair of wings.

Fly

Very pinched waist (between thorax and abdomen) and long narrow body.

Wasp

Behavior to look for:
Flies hover very steadily. Bees do not hover.

Behavior to look for:
May take time collecting flower nectar vs bees which tend to move deliberately and quickly.

Location / GPS: _____ Date _____

Habitat: ◯ Garden ◯ Forest ◯ Woodland ◯ Orchard ◯ Meadow
◯ Other _____

Nest: ◯ Hive ◯ Wood ◯ Tree ◯ Hollow Stem/Reed ◯ Crevice/Edge
◯ Other _____

Climate Type: ◯ Dry ◯ Temperate ◯ Tropical ◯ Other_____

Weather Conditions _____

Color: ◯ Black ◯ Yellow ◯ Brown ◯ White ◯ Blue ◯ Red
◯ Orange ◯ Purple ◯ Green ◯ Striped ◯ (Other) _____

Body: ◯ Round/Chubby ◯ Slender ◯ Furry ◯ (Other) _____

Stinger: ◯ Yes ◯ No

Behavior: ◯ Solitary ◯ Brood ◯ Social ◯ Parasitic ◯ Aggressive
◯ (Other) _____

Notes: _____

Wings →

Head

Antennae

Thorax

Thorax →

Foreleg

Middle Leg

Hindleg

Sketch

a.
Similar to drone but have space between eyes.

b.
Similar to worker but have shorter proboscis.

c.
Have huge eyes that touch top of head.

a. Worker / b. Queen / c. Drone
◯   ◯   ◯

Only female bees have stingers.

♀ All worker bees are female.

Worker

Pollen basket

Queen

♀ Only bee capable of laying fertilized eggs.

Drone bees are the only ♂ male bees in the hive.

Drone

No stingers.

Huge eyes that meet at the top of the head.

Shorty, stubby antennae.

Only one pair of wings.

Fly

Behavior to look for:
Flies hover very steadily. Bees do not hover.

No hairs. Exoskeleton is smooth and brightly colored.

Two pairs of wings (often folded together similar to bees).

Very pinched waist (between thorax and abdomen) and long narrow body.

Wasp

Behavior to look for:
May take time collecting flower nectar vs bees which tend to move deliberately and quickly.

Environment

Location / GPS: _____ Date _____

Habitat: ◯ Garden ◯ Forest ◯ Woodland ◯ Orchard ◯ Meadow
◯ Other _____

Nest: ◯ Hive ◯ Wood ◯ Tree ◯ Hollow Stem/Reed ◯ Crevice/Edge
◯ Other _____

Climate Type: ◯ Dry ◯ Temperate ◯ Tropical ◯ Other_____

Weather Conditions _____

General

Color: ◯ Black ◯ Yellow ◯ Brown ◯ White ◯ Blue ◯ Red
◯ Orange ◯ Purple ◯ Green ◯ Striped ◯(Other) _____

Body: ◯ Round/Chubby ◯ Slender ◯ Furry ◯(Other) _____

Stinger: ◯ Yes ◯ No

Behavior: ◯ Solitary ◯ Brood ◯ Social ◯ Parasitic ◯ Aggressive
◯(Other) _____

Notes: _____

Characteristics

Wings

Head

Antennae

Thorax

Thorax

Foreleg

Middle Leg

Hindleg

Sketch

Head Shape

a.

Similar to drone but have space between eyes.

b.

Similar to worker but have shorter proboscis.

c.

Have huge eyes that touch top of head.

a. <u>Worker</u> / b. <u>Queen</u> / c. <u>Drone</u>
◯ ◯ ◯

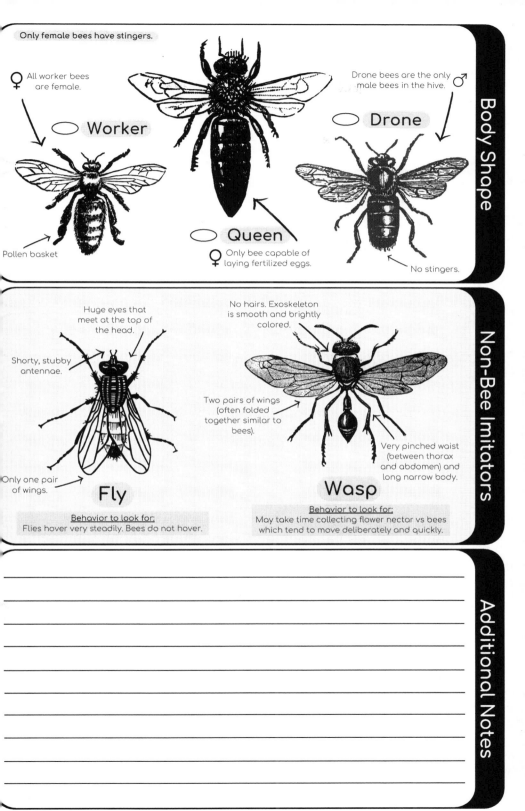

Only female bees have stingers.

All worker bees are female. ♀

Worker

Drone bees are the only male bees in the hive. ♂

Drone

Pollen basket

Queen

♀ Only bee capable of laying fertilized eggs.

No stingers.

Huge eyes that meet at the top of the head.

Shorty, stubby antennae.

Only one pair of wings.

Fly

Behavior to look for:
Flies hover very steadily. Bees do not hover.

No hairs. Exoskeleton is smooth and brightly colored.

Two pairs of wings (often folded together similar to bees).

Very pinched waist (between thorax and abdomen) and long narrow body.

Wasp

Behavior to look for:
May take time collecting flower nectar vs bees which tend to move deliberately and quickly.

Location / GPS: _____ Date _____

Habitat: ○ Garden ○ Forest ○ Woodland ○ Orchard ○ Meadow
         ○ Other _____

Nest: ○ Hive ○ Wood ○ Tree ○ Hollow Stem/Reed ○ Crevice/Edge
      ○ Other _____

Climate Type: ○ Dry ○ Temperate ○ Tropical ○ Other_____

Weather Conditions _____

General

Color: ○ Black ○ Yellow ○ Brown ○ White ○ Blue ○ Red
○ Orange ○ Purple ○ Green ○ Striped ○ (Other) _____

Body: ○ Round/Chubby ○ Slender ○ Furry ○ (Other) _____

Stinger: ○ Yes ○ No

Behavior: ○ Solitary ○ Brood ○ Social ○ Parasitic ○ Aggressive
          ○ (Other) _____

Notes: _____

Characteristics

Wings →
Head
Antennae
Thorax
Foreleg
Middle Leg
Hindleg
Thorax →

Sketch

Head Shape

a. Similar to drone but have space between eyes.

b. Similar to worker but have shorter proboscis.

c. Have huge eyes that touch top of head.

a. **Worker** / b. **Queen** / c. **Drone**
○   ○   ○

Only female bees have stingers.

♀ All worker bees are female.

◯ Worker

Pollen basket

◯ Queen
♀ Only bee capable of laying fertilized eggs.

Drone bees are the only ♂ male bees in the hive.

◯ Drone

No stingers.

Huge eyes that meet at the top of the head.

Shorty, stubby antennae.

Only one pair of wings.

Fly

Behavior to look for:
Flies hover very steadily. Bees do not hover.

No hairs. Exoskeleton is smooth and brightly colored.

Two pairs of wings (often folded together similar to bees).

Very pinched waist (between thorax and abdomen) and long narrow body.

Wasp

Behavior to look for:
May take time collecting flower nectar vs bees which tend to move deliberately and quickly.

Location / GPS: _____ Date _____

Habitat: ◯ Garden ◯ Forest ◯ Woodland ◯ Orchard ◯ Meadow
◯ Other _____

Nest: ◯ Hive ◯ Wood ◯ Tree ◯ Hollow Stem/Reed ◯ Crevice/Edge
◯ Other _____

Climate Type: ◯ Dry ◯ Temperate ◯ Tropical ◯ Other_____

Weather Conditions _____

Color: ◯ Black ◯ Yellow ◯ Brown ◯ White ◯ Blue ◯ Red
◯ Orange ◯ Purple ◯ Green ◯ Striped ◯ (Other) _____

Body: ◯ Round/Chubby ◯ Slender ◯ Furry ◯ (Other) _____

Stinger: ◯ Yes ◯ No

Behavior: ◯ Solitary ◯ Brood ◯ Social ◯ Parasitic ◯ Aggressive
◯ (Other) _____

Notes: _____

Wings → Head
Antennae
Thorax
Thorax → Foreleg
Middle Leg
Hindleg

Sketch

a. Similar to drone but have space between eyes.

b. Similar to worker but have shorter proboscis.

c. Have huge eyes that touch top of head.

a. **Worker** / b. **Queen** / c. **Drone**
◯ ◯ ◯

Only female bees have stingers.

♀ All worker bees are female.

Drone bees are the only male bees in the hive. ♂

◯ Worker

◯ Drone

Pollen basket

◯ Queen

♀ Only bee capable of laying fertilized eggs.

No stingers.

Non-Bee Imitators

Huge eyes that meet at the top of the head.

No hairs. Exoskeleton is smooth and brightly colored.

Shorty, stubby antennae.

Two pairs of wings (often folded together similar to bees).

Very pinched waist (between thorax and abdomen) and long narrow body.

Only one pair of wings.

Fly

Wasp

Behavior to look for:
Flies hover very steadily. Bees do not hover.

Behavior to look for:
May take time collecting flower nectar vs bees which tend to move deliberately and quickly.

Additional Notes

Location / GPS: _____   Date _____

Habitat: ◯ Garden ◯ Forest ◯ Woodland ◯ Orchard ◯ Meadow
◯ Other _____

Nest: ◯ Hive ◯ Wood ◯ Tree ◯ Hollow Stem/Reed ◯ Crevice/Edge
◯ Other _____

Climate Type: ◯ Dry ◯ Temperate ◯ Tropical ◯ Other_____

Weather Conditions _____

Color: ◯ Black ◯ Yellow ◯ Brown ◯ White ◯ Blue ◯ Red
◯ Orange ◯ Purple ◯ Green ◯ Striped ◯ (Other) _____

Body: ◯ Round/Chubby ◯ Slender ◯ Furry ◯ (Other) _____

Stinger: ◯ Yes ◯ No

Behavior: ◯ Solitary ◯ Brood ◯ Social ◯ Parasitic ◯ Aggressive
◯ (Other) _____

Notes: _____

Wings →
Head
Antennae
Thorax
Thorax →
Foreleg
Middle Leg
Hindleg

Sketch

a.
Similar to drone but have space between eyes.

b.
Similar to worker but have shorter proboscis.

c.
Have huge eyes that touch top of head.

a. Worker / b. Queen / c. Drone
◯   ◯   ◯

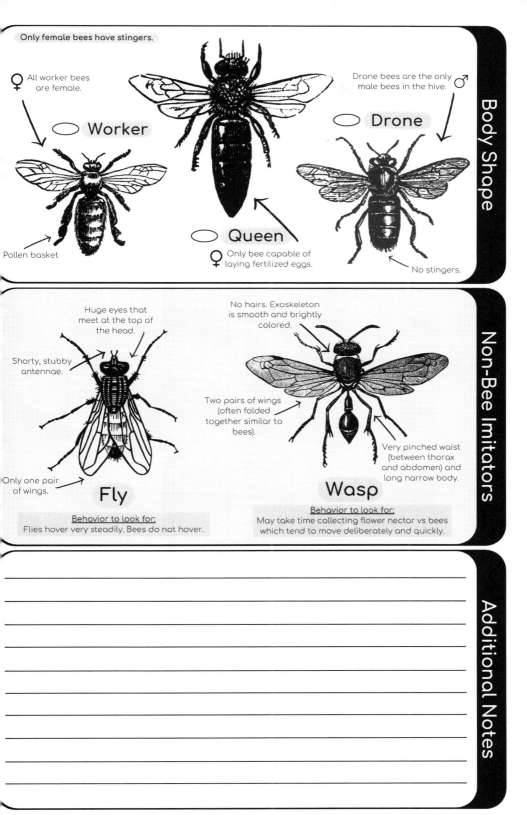

Only female bees have stingers.

All worker bees are female. ♀

Worker

Drone bees are the only male bees in the hive. ♂

Drone

Pollen basket

Queen

Only bee capable of laying fertilized eggs. ♀

No stingers.

Huge eyes that meet at the top of the head.

Shorty, stubby antennae.

No hairs. Exoskeleton is smooth and brightly colored.

Two pairs of wings (often folded together similar to bees).

Only one pair of wings.

Fly

Very pinched waist (between thorax and abdomen) and long narrow body.

Wasp

Behavior to look for:
Flies hover very steadily. Bees do not hover.

Behavior to look for:
May take time collecting flower nectar vs bees which tend to move deliberately and quickly.

Environment

Location / GPS: _____ Date _____

Habitat: ◯ Garden ◯ Forest ◯ Woodland ◯ Orchard ◯ Meadow
◯ Other _____

Nest: ◯ Hive ◯ Wood ◯ Tree ◯ Hollow Stem/Reed ◯ Crevice/Edge
◯ Other _____

Climate Type: ◯ Dry ◯ Temperate ◯ Tropical ◯ Other_____

Weather Conditions _____

General

Color: ◯ Black ◯ Yellow ◯ Brown ◯ White ◯ Blue ◯ Red
◯ Orange ◯ Purple ◯ Green ◯ Striped ◯(Other) _____

Body: ◯ Round/Chubby ◯ Slender ◯ Furry ◯(Other) _____

Stinger: ◯ Yes ◯ No

Behavior: ◯ Solitary ◯ Brood ◯ Social ◯ Parasitic ◯ Aggressive
◯(Other) _____

Notes: _____

Characteristics

Wings →

Head

Antennae

Thorax

Thorax →

Foreleg

Middle Leg

Hindleg

Sketch

Head Shape

a.

Similar to drone but have space between eyes.

b.

Similar to worker but have shorter proboscis.

c.

Have huge eyes that touch top of head.

a. <u>Worker</u> / b. <u>Queen</u> / c. <u>Drone</u>
◯ ◯ ◯

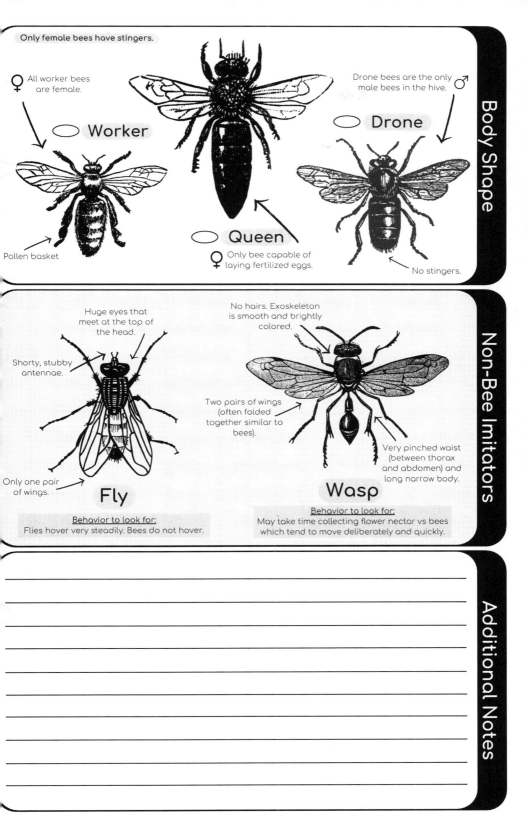

Only female bees have stingers.

All worker bees are female. ♀

Drone bees are the only male bees in the hive. ♂

Worker

Drone

Queen

Pollen basket

♀ Only bee capable of laying fertilized eggs.

No stingers.

Huge eyes that meet at the top of the head.

No hairs. Exoskeleton is smooth and brightly colored.

Shorty, stubby antennae.

Two pairs of wings (often folded together similar to bees).

Only one pair of wings.

Fly

Very pinched waist (between thorax and abdomen) and long narrow body.

Wasp

Behavior to look for:
Flies hover very steadily. Bees do not hover.

Behavior to look for:
May take time collecting flower nectar vs bees which tend to move deliberately and quickly.

Environment

Location / GPS: _____ Date _____

Habitat: ◯ Garden ◯ Forest ◯ Woodland ◯ Orchard ◯ Meadow
◯ Other _____

Nest: ◯ Hive ◯ Wood ◯ Tree ◯ Hollow Stem/Reed ◯ Crevice/Edge
◯ Other _____

Climate Type: ◯ Dry ◯ Temperate ◯ Tropical ◯ Other_____

Weather Conditions _____

General

Color: ◯ Black ◯ Yellow ◯ Brown ◯ White ◯ Blue ◯ Red
◯ Orange ◯ Purple ◯ Green ◯ Striped ◯ (Other) _____

Body: ◯ Round/Chubby ◯ Slender ◯ Furry ◯ (Other) _____

Stinger: ◯ Yes ◯ No

Behavior: ◯ Solitary ◯ Brood ◯ Social ◯ Parasitic ◯ Aggressive
◯ (Other) _____

Notes: _____

Characteristics

Wings
Head
Antennae
Thorax
Thorax
Foreleg
Middle Leg
Hindleg

Sketch

Head Shape

a.
Similar to drone but have space between eyes.

b.
Similar to worker but have shorter proboscis.

c.
Have huge eyes that touch top of head.

a. <u>Worker</u> / b. <u>Queen</u> / c. <u>Drone</u>
◯   ◯   ◯

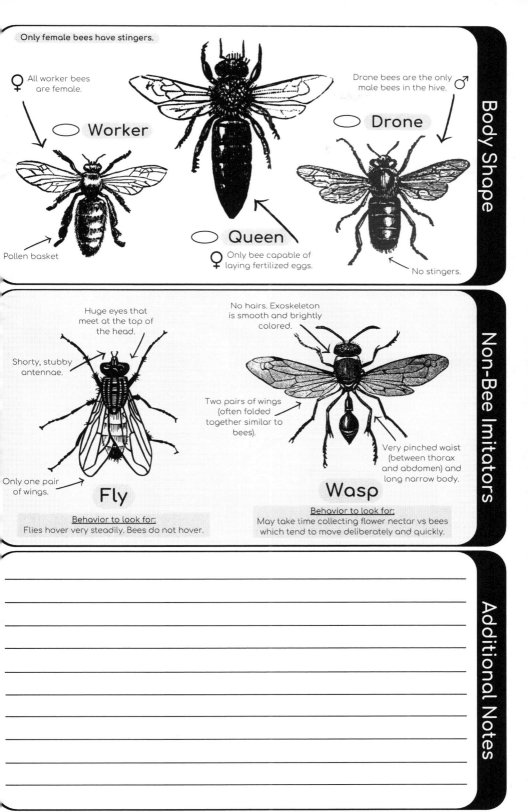

Only female bees have stingers.

All worker bees are female.

Worker

Drone bees are the only male bees in the hive.

Drone

Pollen basket

Queen

Only bee capable of laying fertilized eggs.

No stingers.

Body Shape

Huge eyes that meet at the top of the head.

Shorty, stubby antennae.

No hairs. Exoskeleton is smooth and brightly colored.

Two pairs of wings (often folded together similar to bees).

Only one pair of wings.

Fly

Behavior to look for:
Flies hover very steadily. Bees do not hover.

Very pinched waist (between thorax and abdomen) and long narrow body.

Wasp

Behavior to look for:
May take time collecting flower nectar vs bees which tend to move deliberately and quickly.

Non-Bee Imitators

Additional Notes

Location / GPS: _____ Date _____

Habitat: ⭘ Garden ⭘ Forest ⭘ Woodland ⭘ Orchard ⭘ Meadow
⭘ Other _____

Nest: ⭘ Hive ⭘ Wood ⭘ Tree ⭘ Hollow Stem/Reed ⭘ Crevice/Edge
⭘ Other _____

Climate Type: ⭘ Dry ⭘ Temperate ⭘ Tropical ⭘ Other_____

Weather Conditions _____

Color: ⭘ Black ⭘ Yellow ⭘ Brown ⭘ White ⭘ Blue ⭘ Red
⭘ Orange ⭘ Purple ⭘ Green ⭘ Striped ⭘ (Other) _____

Body: ⭘ Round/Chubby ⭘ Slender ⭘ Furry ⭘ (Other) _____

Stinger: ⭘ Yes ⭘ No

Behavior: ⭘ Solitary ⭘ Brood ⭘ Social ⭘ Parasitic ⭘ Aggressive
⭘ (Other) _____

Notes: _____

Wings
Head
Antennae
Thorax
Thorax
Foreleg
Middle Leg
Hindleg

Sketch

a.
Similar to drone but have space between eyes.

b.
Similar to worker but have shorter proboscis.

c.
Have huge eyes that touch top of head.

a. **Worker** / b. **Queen** / c. **Drone**
⭘ ⭘ ⭘

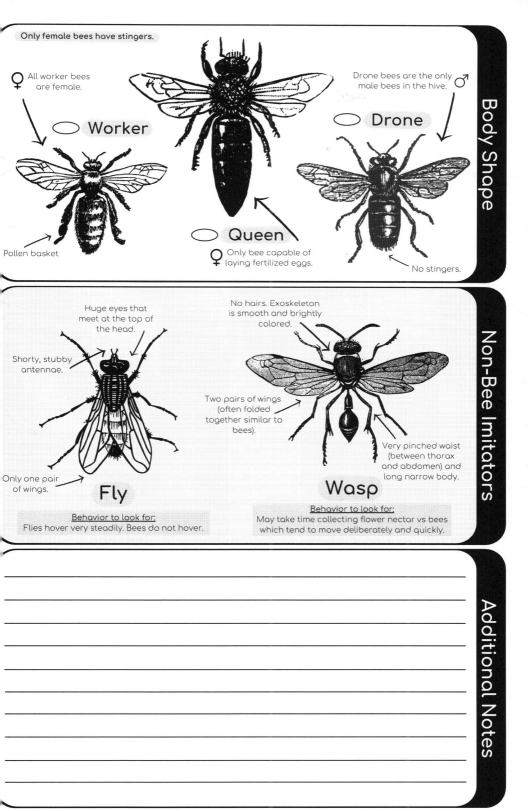

Only female bees have stingers.

All worker bees are female. ♀

Worker

Drone bees are the only male bees in the hive. ♂

Drone

Pollen basket

Queen

♀ Only bee capable of laying fertilized eggs.

No stingers.

Huge eyes that meet at the top of the head.

No hairs. Exoskeleton is smooth and brightly colored.

Shorty, stubby antennae.

Two pairs of wings (often folded together similar to bees).

Very pinched waist (between thorax and abdomen) and long narrow body.

Only one pair of wings.

Fly

Wasp

Behavior to look for:
Flies hover very steadily. Bees do not hover.

Behavior to look for:
May take time collecting flower nectar vs bees which tend to move deliberately and quickly.

Environment

Location / GPS: _____ Date _____

Habitat: ○ Garden ○ Forest ○ Woodland ○ Orchard ○ Meadow
○ Other _____

Nest: ○ Hive ○ Wood ○ Tree ○ Hollow Stem/Reed ○ Crevice/Edge
○ Other _____

Climate Type: ○ Dry ○ Temperate ○ Tropical ○ Other_____

Weather Conditions _____

General

Color: ○ Black ○ Yellow ○ Brown ○ White ○ Blue ○ Red
○ Orange ○ Purple ○ Green ○ Striped ○ (Other) _____

Body: ○ Round/Chubby ○ Slender ○ Furry ○ (Other) _____

Stinger: ○ Yes ○ No

Behavior: ○ Solitary ○ Brood ○ Social ○ Parasitic ○ Aggressive
○ (Other) _____

Notes: _____

Characteristics

Wings →

Head

Antennae

Thorax

Thorax →

← Foreleg

Middle Leg

Hindleg

Sketch

Head Shape

a. Similar to drone but have space between eyes.

b. Similar to worker but have shorter proboscis.

c. Have huge eyes that touch top of head.

a. **Worker** / b. **Queen** / c. **Drone**
○   ○   ○

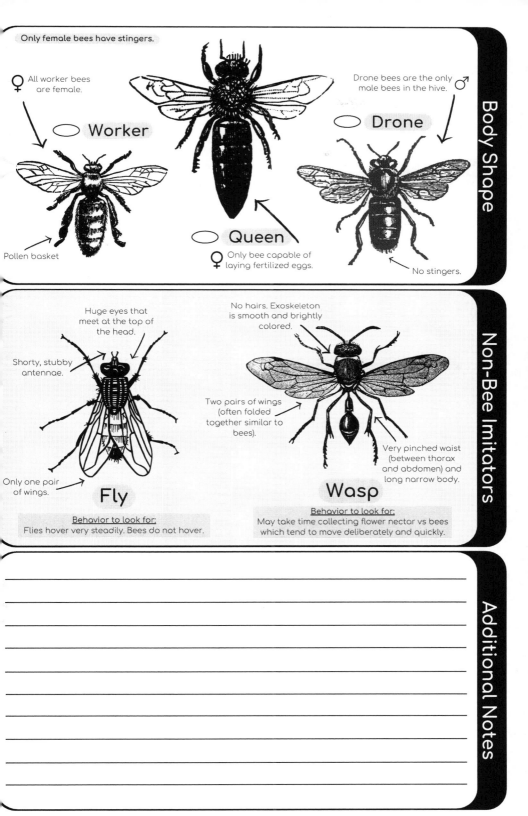

Only female bees have stingers.

♀ All worker bees are female.

◯ Worker

Drone bees are the only male bees in the hive. ♂

◯ Drone

Pollen basket

◯ Queen

♀ Only bee capable of laying fertilized eggs.

No stingers.

Huge eyes that meet at the top of the head.

No hairs. Exoskeleton is smooth and brightly colored.

Shorty, stubby antennae.

Two pairs of wings (often folded together similar to bees).

Very pinched waist (between thorax and abdomen) and long narrow body.

Only one pair of wings.

Fly

Wasp

Behavior to look for:
Flies hover very steadily. Bees do not hover.

Behavior to look for:
May take time collecting flower nectar vs bees which tend to move deliberately and quickly.

Location / GPS: _____ Date _____

Habitat: ◯ Garden ◯ Forest ◯ Woodland ◯ Orchard ◯ Meadow
◯ Other _____

Nest: ◯ Hive ◯ Wood ◯ Tree ◯ Hollow Stem/Reed ◯ Crevice/Edge
◯ Other _____

Climate Type: ◯ Dry ◯ Temperate ◯ Tropical ◯ Other_____

Weather Conditions _____

Color: ◯ Black ◯ Yellow ◯ Brown ◯ White ◯ Blue ◯ Red
◯ Orange ◯ Purple ◯ Green ◯ Striped ◯(Other) _____

Body: ◯ Round/Chubby ◯ Slender ◯ Furry ◯(Other) _____

Stinger: ◯ Yes ◯ No

Behavior: ◯ Solitary ◯ Brood ◯ Social ◯ Parasitic ◯ Aggressive
◯(Other) _____

Notes: _____

Wings — Head — Antennae — Thorax — Foreleg — Middle Leg — Hindleg — Thorax

Sketch

a.
Similar to drone but have space between eyes.

b.
Similar to worker but have shorter proboscis.

c.
Have huge eyes that touch top of head.

a. Worker / b. Queen / c. Drone
◯ ◯ ◯

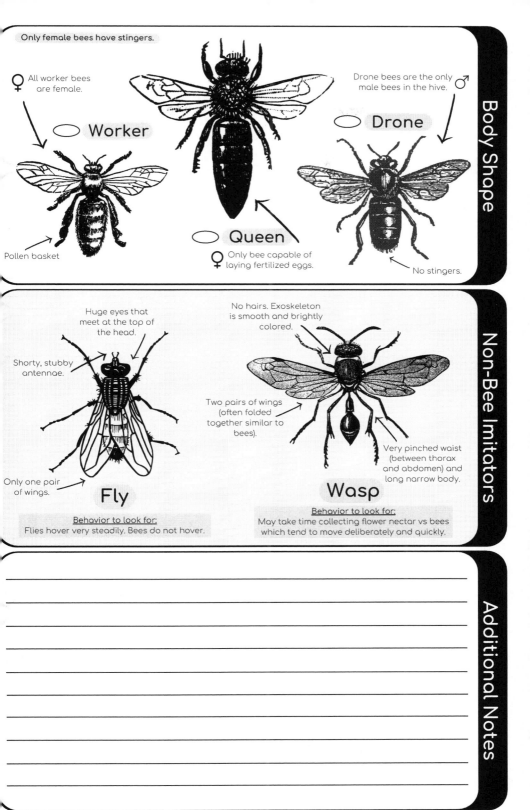

Only female bees have stingers.

♀ All worker bees are female.

Worker

Drone bees are the only male bees in the hive. ♂

Drone

Pollen basket

Queen

♀ Only bee capable of laying fertilized eggs.

No stingers.

Huge eyes that meet at the top of the head.

No hairs. Exoskeleton is smooth and brightly colored.

Shorty, stubby antennae.

Two pairs of wings (often folded together similar to bees).

Only one pair of wings.

Fly

Very pinched waist (between thorax and abdomen) and long narrow body.

Wasp

Behavior to look for:
Flies hover very steadily. Bees do not hover.

Behavior to look for:
May take time collecting flower nectar vs bees which tend to move deliberately and quickly.

Environment

Location / GPS: _____ Date _____

Habitat: ○ Garden ○ Forest ○ Woodland ○ Orchard ○ Meadow
○ Other _____

Nest: ○ Hive ○ Wood ○ Tree ○ Hollow Stem/Reed ○ Crevice/Edge
○ Other _____

Climate Type: ○ Dry ○ Temperate ○ Tropical ○ Other_____

Weather Conditions _____

General

Color: ○ Black ○ Yellow ○ Brown ○ White ○ Blue ○ Red
○ Orange ○ Purple ○ Green ○ Striped ○ (Other) _____

Body: ○ Round/Chubby ○ Slender ○ Furry ○ (Other) _____

Stinger: ○ Yes ○ No

Behavior: ○ Solitary ○ Brood ○ Social ○ Parasitic ○ Aggressive
○ (Other) _____

Notes: _____

Characteristics

Wings

Head

Antennae

Thorax

Thorax

Foreleg

Middle Leg

Hindleg

Sketch

Head Shape

a. Similar to drone but have space between eyes.

b. Similar to worker but have shorter proboscis.

c. Have huge eyes that touch top of head.

a. **Worker** / b. **Queen** / c. **Drone**
○   ○   ○

Only female bees have stingers.

All worker bees are female.

Worker

Drone bees are the only male bees in the hive.

Drone

Queen

Only bee capable of laying fertilized eggs.

Pollen basket

No stingers.

Huge eyes that meet at the top of the head.

Shorty, stubby antennae.

No hairs. Exoskeleton is smooth and brightly colored.

Two pairs of wings (often folded together similar to bees).

Only one pair of wings.

Fly

Behavior to look for:
Flies hover very steadily. Bees do not hover.

Very pinched waist (between thorax and abdomen) and long narrow body.

Wasp

Behavior to look for:
May take time collecting flower nectar vs bees which tend to move deliberately and quickly.

Location / GPS: _____ Date _____

Habitat: ◯ Garden ◯ Forest ◯ Woodland ◯ Orchard ◯ Meadow
◯ Other _____

Nest: ◯ Hive ◯ Wood ◯ Tree ◯ Hollow Stem/Reed ◯ Crevice/Edge
◯ Other _____

Climate Type: ◯ Dry ◯ Temperate ◯ Tropical ◯ Other_____
Weather Conditions _____

Color: ◯ Black ◯ Yellow ◯ Brown ◯ White ◯ Blue ◯ Red
◯ Orange ◯ Purple ◯ Green ◯ Striped ◯(Other) _____
Body: ◯ Round/Chubby ◯ Slender ◯ Furry ◯(Other) _____
Stinger: ◯ Yes ◯ No
Behavior: ◯ Solitary ◯ Brood ◯ Social ◯ Parasitic ◯ Aggressive
◯(Other) _____

Notes: _____

Wings
Head
Antennae
Thorax
Thorax
Foreleg
Middle Leg
Hindleg

Sketch

a.
Similar to drone but have space between eyes.

b.
Similar to worker but have shorter proboscis.

c.
Have huge eyes that touch top of head.

a. Worker / b. Queen / c. Drone

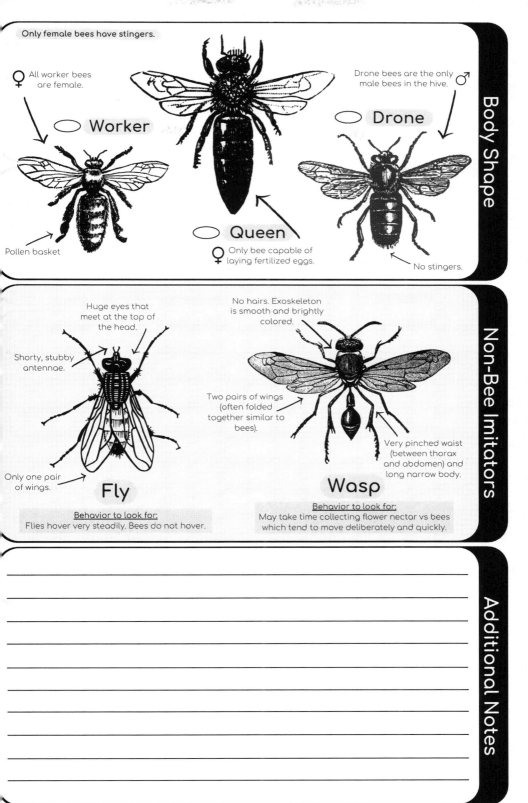

Only female bees have stingers.

♀ All worker bees are female.

Drone bees are the only male bees in the hive. ♂

Worker

Drone

Queen

Pollen basket

♀ Only bee capable of laying fertilized eggs.

No stingers.

Huge eyes that meet at the top of the head.

No hairs. Exoskeleton is smooth and brightly colored.

Shorty, stubby antennae.

Two pairs of wings (often folded together similar to bees).

Only one pair of wings.

Fly

Very pinched waist (between thorax and abdomen) and long narrow body.

Wasp

Behavior to look for:
Flies hover very steadily. Bees do not hover.

Behavior to look for:
May take time collecting flower nectar vs bees which tend to move deliberately and quickly.

Location / GPS: _____ Date _____

Habitat: ◯ Garden ◯ Forest ◯ Woodland ◯ Orchard ◯ Meadow
         ◯ Other _____

Nest: ◯ Hive ◯ Wood ◯ Tree ◯ Hollow Stem/Reed ◯ Crevice/Edge
      ◯ Other _____

Climate Type: ◯ Dry ◯ Temperate ◯ Tropical ◯ Other_____
Weather Conditions _____

Color: ◯ Black ◯ Yellow ◯ Brown ◯White ◯ Blue ◯ Red
       ◯ Orange ◯ Purple ◯ Green ◯ Striped ◯(Other) _____
Body: ◯ Round/Chubby ◯ Slender ◯ Furry ◯(Other) _____
Stinger: ◯ Yes ◯ No
Behavior: ◯ Solitary ◯ Brood ◯ Social ◯ Parasitic ◯ Aggressive
          ◯(Other) _____
Notes: _____

Wings —
Head
Antennae
Thorax
Foreleg
Middle Leg
Hindleg
Thorax

Sketch

a.
Similar to drone but have space between eyes.

b.
Similar to worker but have shorter proboscis.

c.
Have huge eyes that touch top of head.

a. Worker / b. Queen / c. Drone
◯   ◯   ◯

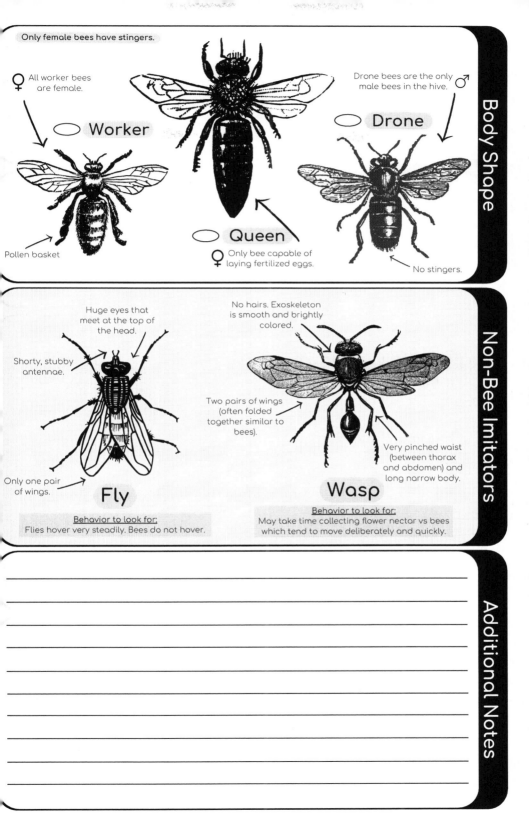

Only female bees have stingers.

Body Shape

All worker bees are female.

Worker

Pollen basket

Queen

Only bee capable of laying fertilized eggs.

Drone bees are the only male bees in the hive.

Drone

No stingers.

Non-Bee Imitators

Huge eyes that meet at the top of the head.

Shorty, stubby antennae.

Only one pair of wings.

Fly

Behavior to look for:
Flies hover very steadily. Bees do not hover.

No hairs. Exoskeleton is smooth and brightly colored.

Two pairs of wings (often folded together similar to bees).

Very pinched waist (between thorax and abdomen) and long narrow body.

Wasp

Behavior to look for:
May take time collecting flower nectar vs bees which tend to move deliberately and quickly.

Additional Notes

Environment

Location / GPS: _____ Date _____

Habitat: ◯ Garden ◯ Forest ◯ Woodland ◯ Orchard ◯ Meadow
◯ Other _____

Nest: ◯ Hive ◯ Wood ◯ Tree ◯ Hollow Stem/Reed ◯ Crevice/Edge
◯ Other _____

Climate Type: ◯ Dry ◯ Temperate ◯ Tropical ◯ Other_____

Weather Conditions _____

General

Color: ◯ Black ◯ Yellow ◯ Brown ◯ White ◯ Blue ◯ Red
◯ Orange ◯ Purple ◯ Green ◯ Striped ◯ (Other) _____

Body: ◯ Round/Chubby ◯ Slender ◯ Furry ◯ (Other) _____

Stinger: ◯ Yes ◯ No

Behavior: ◯ Solitary ◯ Brood ◯ Social ◯ Parasitic ◯ Aggressive
◯ (Other) _____

Notes: _____

Characteristics

Wings

Head

Antennae

Thorax

Thorax

Foreleg

Middle Leg

Hindleg

Sketch

Head Shape

a.
Similar to drone but have space between eyes.

b.
Similar to worker but have shorter proboscis.

c.
Have huge eyes that touch top of head.

a. Worker / b. Queen / c. Drone
◯   ◯   ◯

Only female bees have stingers.

All worker bees are female. ♀

Drone bees are the only male bees in the hive. ♂

⬭ Worker

⬭ Drone

Pollen basket

⬭ Queen

Only bee capable of ♀ laying fertilized eggs.

No stingers.

Huge eyes that meet at the top of the head.

Shorty, stubby antennae.

No hairs. Exoskeleton is smooth and brightly colored.

Two pairs of wings (often folded together similar to bees).

Only one pair of wings.

Fly

Very pinched waist (between thorax and abdomen) and long narrow body.

Wasp

Behavior to look for:
Flies hover very steadily. Bees do not hover.

Behavior to look for:
May take time collecting flower nectar vs bees which tend to move deliberately and quickly.

Location / GPS: _____ Date _____

Habitat: ◯ Garden ◯ Forest ◯ Woodland ◯ Orchard ◯ Meadow
◯ Other _____

Nest: ◯ Hive ◯ Wood ◯ Tree ◯ Hollow Stem/Reed ◯ Crevice/Edge
◯ Other _____

Climate Type: ◯ Dry ◯ Temperate ◯ Tropical ◯ Other_____

Weather Conditions _____

Color: ◯ Black ◯ Yellow ◯ Brown ◯ White ◯ Blue ◯ Red
◯ Orange ◯ Purple ◯ Green ◯ Striped ◯ (Other) _____

Body: ◯ Round/Chubby ◯ Slender ◯ Furry ◯ (Other) _____

Stinger: ◯ Yes ◯ No

Behavior: ◯ Solitary ◯ Brood ◯ Social ◯ Parasitic ◯ Aggressive
◯ (Other) _____

Notes: _____

Wings →
Head
Antennae
Thorax
Foreleg
Thorax →
Middle Leg
Hindleg

Sketch

a.
Similar to drone but have space between eyes.

b.
Similar to worker but have shorter proboscis.

c.
Have huge eyes that touch top of head.

a. Worker / b. Queen / c. Drone
◯   ◯   ◯

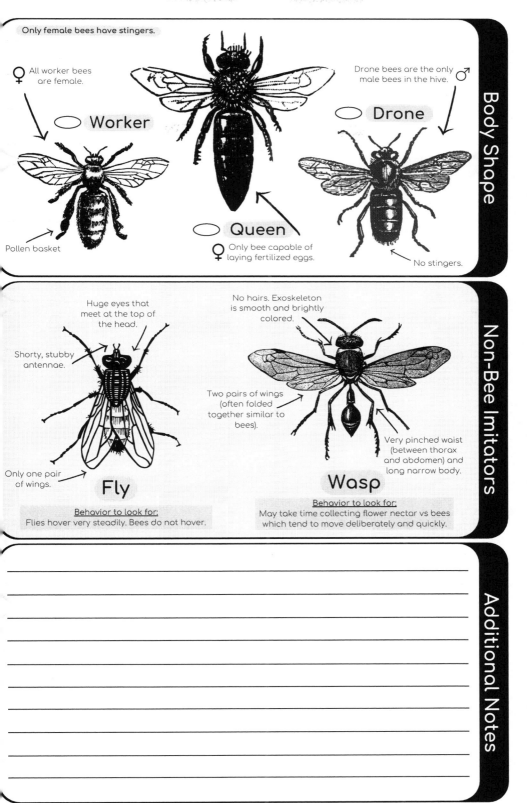

Only female bees have stingers.

♀ All worker bees are female.

Drone bees are the only male bees in the hive. ♂

◯ Worker

◯ Drone

Pollen basket

◯ Queen

♀ Only bee capable of laying fertilized eggs.

No stingers.

Huge eyes that meet at the top of the head.

No hairs. Exoskeleton is smooth and brightly colored.

Shorty, stubby antennae.

Two pairs of wings (often folded together similar to bees).

Only one pair of wings.

Fly

Very pinched waist (between thorax and abdomen) and long narrow body.

Wasp

Behavior to look for:
Flies hover very steadily. Bees do not hover.

Behavior to look for:
May take time collecting flower nectar vs bees which tend to move deliberately and quickly.

Environment

Location / GPS: _____ Date _____

Habitat: ◯ Garden ◯ Forest ◯ Woodland ◯ Orchard ◯ Meadow
◯ Other _____

Nest: ◯ Hive ◯ Wood ◯ Tree ◯ Hollow Stem/Reed ◯ Crevice/Edge
◯ Other _____

Climate Type: ◯ Dry ◯ Temperate ◯ Tropical ◯ Other _____

Weather Conditions _____

General

Color: ◯ Black ◯ Yellow ◯ Brown ◯ White ◯ Blue ◯ Red
◯ Orange ◯ Purple ◯ Green ◯ Striped ◯ (Other) _____

Body: ◯ Round/Chubby ◯ Slender ◯ Furry ◯ (Other) _____

Stinger: ◯ Yes ◯ No

Behavior: ◯ Solitary ◯ Brood ◯ Social ◯ Parasitic ◯ Aggressive
◯ (Other) _____

Notes: _____

Characteristics

Wings → Head
Antennae
Thorax
Thorax → Foreleg
Middle Leg
Hindleg

Sketch

Head Shape

a. Similar to drone but have space between eyes.

b. Similar to worker but have shorter proboscis.

c. Have huge eyes that touch top of head.

a. **Worker** / b. **Queen** / c. **Drone**
◯ ◯ ◯

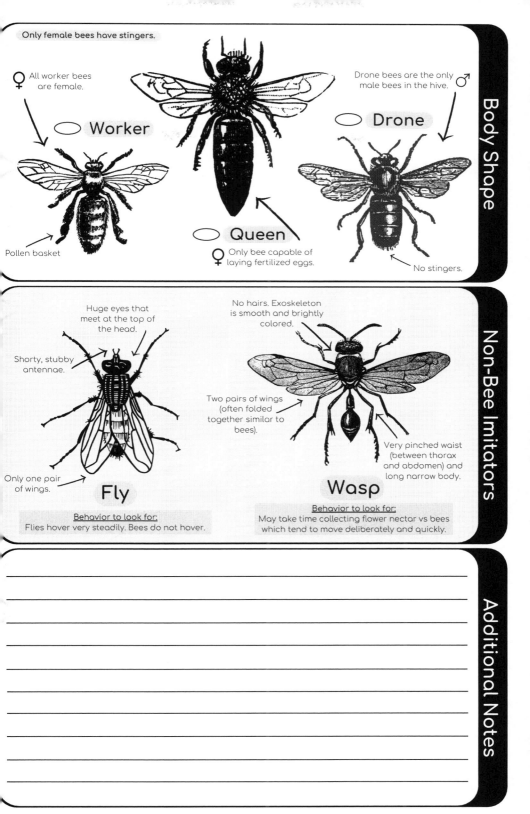

Only female bees have stingers.

All worker bees are female. ♀

Drone bees are the only male bees in the hive. ♂

Worker

Drone

Pollen basket

Queen

Only bee capable of laying fertilized eggs. ♀

No stingers.

Huge eyes that meet at the top of the head.

No hairs. Exoskeleton is smooth and brightly colored.

Shorty, stubby antennae.

Two pairs of wings (often folded together similar to bees).

Only one pair of wings.

Fly

Wasp

Very pinched waist (between thorax and abdomen) and long narrow body.

Behavior to look for:
Flies hover very steadily. Bees do not hover.

Behavior to look for:
May take time collecting flower nectar vs bees which tend to move deliberately and quickly.

Location / GPS: _____ **Date** _____

Habitat: ◯ Garden ◯ Forest ◯ Woodland ◯ Orchard ◯ Meadow
◯ Other _____

Nest: ◯ Hive ◯ Wood ◯ Tree ◯ Hollow Stem/Reed ◯ Crevice/Edge
◯ Other _____

Climate Type: ◯ Dry ◯ Temperate ◯ Tropical ◯ Other _____

Weather Conditions _____

Color: ◯ Black ◯ Yellow ◯ Brown ◯ White ◯ Blue ◯ Red
◯ Orange ◯ Purple ◯ Green ◯ Striped ◯ (Other) _____

Body: ◯ Round/Chubby ◯ Slender ◯ Furry ◯ (Other) _____

Stinger: ◯ Yes ◯ No

Behavior: ◯ Solitary ◯ Brood ◯ Social ◯ Parasitic ◯ Aggressive
◯ (Other) _____

Notes: _____

Wings
Head
Antennae
Thorax
Foreleg
Middle Leg
Hindleg
Thorax

Sketch

a. Similar to drone but have space between eyes.

b. Similar to worker but have shorter proboscis.

c. Have huge eyes that touch top of head.

a. Worker / **b. Queen** / **c. Drone**
◯   ◯   ◯

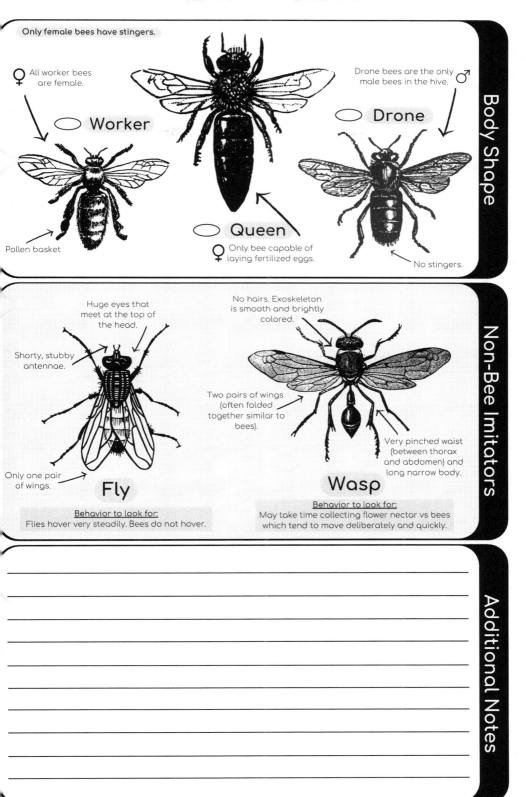

Only female bees have stingers.

♀ All worker bees are female.

○ Worker

Pollen basket

○ Queen
♀ Only bee capable of laying fertilized eggs.

Drone bees are the only male bees in the hive. ♂

○ Drone

No stingers.

Huge eyes that meet at the top of the head.

Shorty, stubby antennae.

Only one pair of wings.

Fly

Behavior to look for:
Flies hover very steadily. Bees do not hover.

No hairs. Exoskeleton is smooth and brightly colored.

Two pairs of wings (often folded together similar to bees).

Very pinched waist (between thorax and abdomen) and long narrow body.

Wasp

Behavior to look for:
May take time collecting flower nectar vs bees which tend to move deliberately and quickly.

Location / GPS: _____ Date _____

Habitat: ◯ Garden ◯ Forest ◯ Woodland ◯ Orchard ◯ Meadow
◯ Other _____

Nest: ◯ Hive ◯ Wood ◯ Tree ◯ Hollow Stem/Reed ◯ Crevice/Edge
◯ Other _____

Climate Type: ◯ Dry ◯ Temperate ◯ Tropical ◯ Other _____

Weather Conditions _____

Color: ◯ Black ◯ Yellow ◯ Brown ◯ White ◯ Blue ◯ Red
◯ Orange ◯ Purple ◯ Green ◯ Striped ◯ (Other) _____

Body: ◯ Round/Chubby ◯ Slender ◯ Furry ◯ (Other) _____

Stinger: ◯ Yes ◯ No

Behavior: ◯ Solitary ◯ Brood ◯ Social ◯ Parasitic ◯ Aggressive
◯ (Other) _____

Notes: _____

Wings
Head
Antennae
Thorax
Thorax
Foreleg
Middle Leg
Hindleg

Sketch

a. Similar to drone but have space between eyes.

b. Similar to worker but have shorter proboscis.

c. Have huge eyes that touch top of head.

a. **Worker** / b. **Queen** / c. **Drone**
◯   ◯   ◯

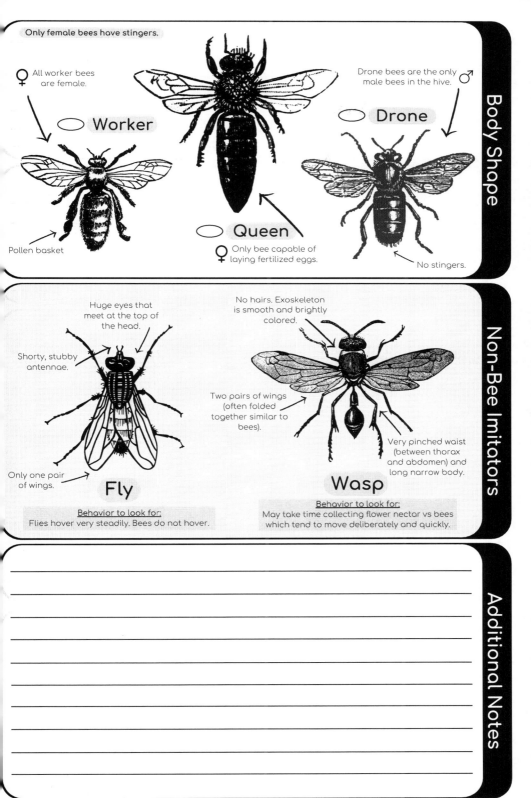

Only female bees have stingers.

♀ All worker bees are female.

◯ Worker

Pollen basket

Drone bees are the only male bees in the hive. ♂

◯ Drone

No stingers.

◯ Queen

♀ Only bee capable of laying fertilized eggs.

Huge eyes that meet at the top of the head.

Shorty, stubby antennae.

Only one pair of wings.

Fly

Behavior to look for:
Flies hover very steadily. Bees do not hover.

No hairs. Exoskeleton is smooth and brightly colored.

Two pairs of wings (often folded together similar to bees).

Very pinched waist (between thorax and abdomen) and long narrow body.

Wasp

Behavior to look for:
May take time collecting flower nectar vs bees which tend to move deliberately and quickly.

Location / GPS: _____ Date _____

Habitat: ◯ Garden ◯ Forest ◯ Woodland ◯ Orchard ◯ Meadow
◯ Other _____

Nest: ◯ Hive ◯ Wood ◯ Tree ◯ Hollow Stem/Reed ◯ Crevice/Edge
◯ Other _____

Climate Type: ◯ Dry ◯ Temperate ◯ Tropical ◯ Other _____

Weather Conditions _____

General

Color: ◯ Black ◯ Yellow ◯ Brown ◯ White ◯ Blue ◯ Red
◯ Orange ◯ Purple ◯ Green ◯ Striped ◯ (Other) _____

Body: ◯ Round/Chubby ◯ Slender ◯ Furry ◯ (Other) _____

Stinger: ◯ Yes ◯ No

Behavior: ◯ Solitary ◯ Brood ◯ Social ◯ Parasitic ◯ Aggressive
◯ (Other) _____

Notes: _____

Characteristics

Wings

Head

Antennae

Thorax

Thorax

Foreleg

Middle Leg

Hindleg

Sketch

Head Shape

a. Similar to drone but have space between eyes.

b. Similar to worker but have shorter proboscis.

c. Have huge eyes that touch top of head.

a. **Worker** / b. **Queen** / c. **Drone**
◯ ◯ ◯

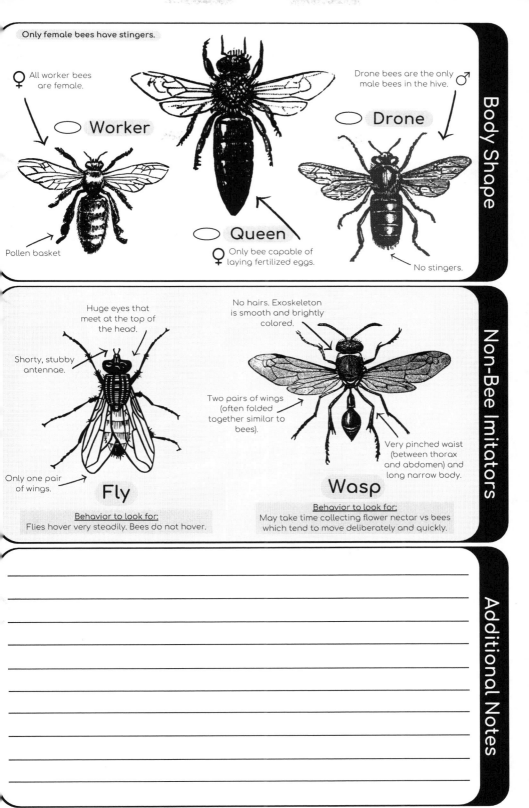

Only female bees have stingers.

♀ All worker bees are female.

○ Worker

Drone bees are the only ♂ male bees in the hive.

○ Drone

Pollen basket

○ Queen

♀ Only bee capable of laying fertilized eggs.

No stingers.

Huge eyes that meet at the top of the head.

Shorty, stubby antennae.

No hairs. Exoskeleton is smooth and brightly colored.

Two pairs of wings (often folded together similar to bees).

Only one pair of wings.

Fly

Very pinched waist (between thorax and abdomen) and long narrow body.

Wasp

Behavior to look for:
Flies hover very steadily. Bees do not hover.

Behavior to look for:
May take time collecting flower nectar vs bees which tend to move deliberately and quickly.

Location / GPS: _____ Date _____

Habitat: ◯ Garden ◯ Forest ◯ Woodland ◯ Orchard ◯ Meadow
         ◯ Other _____

Nest: ◯ Hive ◯ Wood ◯ Tree ◯ Hollow Stem/Reed ◯ Crevice/Edge
       ◯ Other _____

Climate Type: ◯ Dry ◯ Temperate ◯ Tropical ◯ Other_____
Weather Conditions _____

Color: ◯ Black ◯ Yellow ◯ Brown ◯ White ◯ Blue ◯ Red
        ◯ Orange ◯ Purple ◯ Green ◯ Striped ◯ (Other) _____

Body: ◯ Round/Chubby ◯ Slender ◯ Furry ◯ (Other) _____

Stinger: ◯ Yes ◯ No

Behavior: ◯ Solitary ◯ Brood ◯ Social ◯ Parasitic ◯ Aggressive
           ◯ (Other) _____

Notes: _____

Wings
Head
Antennae
Thorax
Thorax
Foreleg
Middle Leg
Hindleg

Sketch

a. Similar to drone but have space between eyes.

b. Similar to worker but have shorter proboscis.

c. Have huge eyes that touch top of head.

a. **Worker** / b. **Queen** / c. **Drone**
◯   ◯   ◯

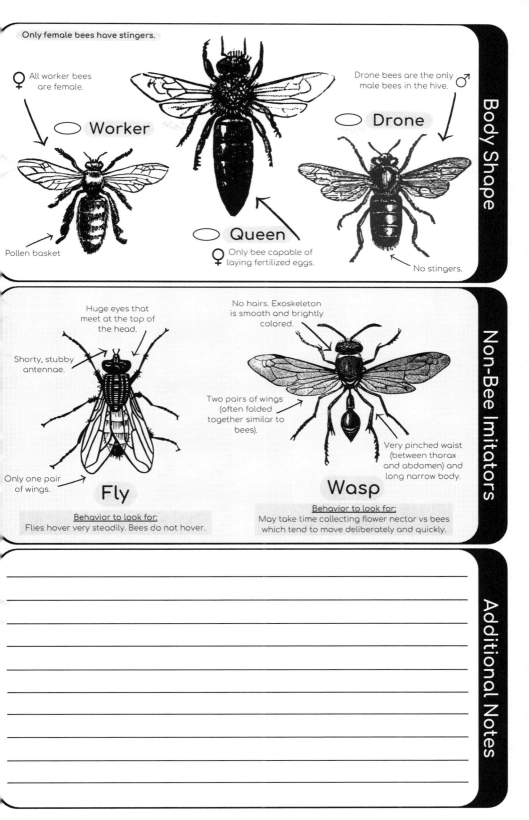

Only female bees have stingers.

♀ All worker bees are female.

Worker

Drone bees are the only male bees in the hive. ♂

Drone

Pollen basket

Queen

♀ Only bee capable of laying fertilized eggs.

No stingers.

Huge eyes that meet at the top of the head.

Shorty, stubby antennae.

No hairs. Exoskeleton is smooth and brightly colored.

Two pairs of wings (often folded together similar to bees).

Only one pair of wings.

Fly

Behavior to look for:
Flies hover very steadily. Bees do not hover.

Very pinched waist (between thorax and abdomen) and long narrow body.

Wasp

Behavior to look for:
May take time collecting flower nectar vs bees which tend to move deliberately and quickly.

Location / GPS: _____ Date _____

Habitat: ◯ Garden ◯ Forest ◯ Woodland ◯ Orchard ◯ Meadow
◯ Other _____

Nest: ◯ Hive ◯ Wood ◯ Tree ◯ Hollow Stem/Reed ◯ Crevice/Edge
◯ Other _____

Climate Type: ◯ Dry ◯ Temperate ◯ Tropical ◯ Other_____

Weather Conditions _____

Color: ◯ Black ◯ Yellow ◯ Brown ◯ White ◯ Blue ◯ Red
◯ Orange ◯ Purple ◯ Green ◯ Striped ◯ (Other) _____

Body: ◯ Round/Chubby ◯ Slender ◯ Furry ◯ (Other) _____

Stinger: ◯ Yes ◯ No

Behavior: ◯ Solitary ◯ Brood ◯ Social ◯ Parasitic ◯ Aggressive
◯ (Other) _____

Notes: _____

Wings — Head

Antennae

Thorax

Thorax — Foreleg

Middle Leg

Hindleg

Sketch

a. Similar to drone but have space between eyes.

b.

c. Have huge eyes that touch top of head.

Similar to worker but have shorter proboscis.

a. <u>Worker</u> / b. <u>Queen</u> / c. <u>Drone</u>
◯ ◯ ◯

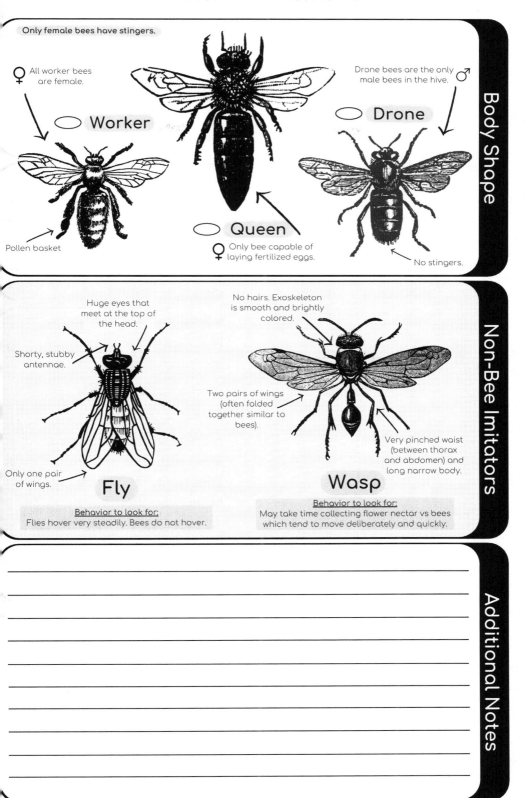

Only female bees have stingers.

♀ All worker bees are female.

○ Worker

Pollen basket

○ Queen

♀ Only bee capable of laying fertilized eggs.

Drone bees are the only male bees in the hive. ♂

○ Drone

No stingers.

Huge eyes that meet at the top of the head.

Shorty, stubby antennae.

Only one pair of wings.

Fly

No hairs. Exoskeleton is smooth and brightly colored.

Two pairs of wings (often folded together similar to bees).

Very pinched waist (between thorax and abdomen) and long narrow body.

Wasp

Behavior to look for:
Flies hover very steadily. Bees do not hover.

Behavior to look for:
May take time collecting flower nectar vs bees which tend to move deliberately and quickly.

Location / GPS: _____ Date _____

Habitat: ◯ Garden ◯ Forest ◯ Woodland ◯ Orchard ◯ Meadow
◯ Other _____

Nest: ◯ Hive ◯ Wood ◯ Tree ◯ Hollow Stem/Reed ◯ Crevice/Edge
◯ Other _____

Climate Type: ◯ Dry ◯ Temperate ◯ Tropical ◯ Other_____

Weather Conditions _____

Color: ◯ Black ◯ Yellow ◯ Brown ◯ White ◯ Blue ◯ Red
◯ Orange ◯ Purple ◯ Green ◯ Striped ◯ (Other) _____

Body: ◯ Round/Chubby ◯ Slender ◯ Furry ◯ (Other) _____

Stinger: ◯ Yes ◯ No

Behavior: ◯ Solitary ◯ Brood ◯ Social ◯ Parasitic ◯ Aggressive
◯ (Other) _____

Notes: _____

Wings →
Head
Antennae
Thorax
Thorax →
Foreleg
Middle Leg
Hindleg

Sketch

a.
Similar to drone but have space between eyes.

b.
Similar to worker but have shorter proboscis.

c.
Have huge eyes that touch top of head.

a. Worker / b. Queen / c. Drone
◯ ◯ ◯

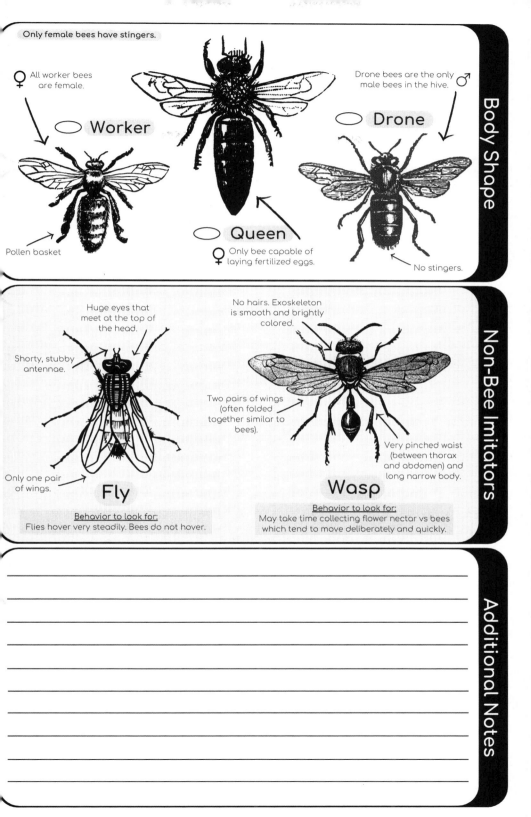

Only female bees have stingers.

All worker bees are female.

Worker

Pollen basket

Queen
Only bee capable of laying fertilized eggs.

Drone bees are the only male bees in the hive.

Drone

No stingers.

Huge eyes that meet at the top of the head.

Shorty, stubby antennae.

Only one pair of wings.

Fly

Behavior to look for:
Flies hover very steadily. Bees do not hover.

No hairs. Exoskeleton is smooth and brightly colored.

Two pairs of wings (often folded together similar to bees).

Very pinched waist (between thorax and abdomen) and long narrow body.

Wasp

Behavior to look for:
May take time collecting flower nectar vs bees which tend to move deliberately and quickly.

Location / GPS: _____ Date _____

Habitat: ◯ Garden ◯ Forest ◯ Woodland ◯ Orchard ◯ Meadow
◯ Other _____

Nest: ◯ Hive ◯ Wood ◯ Tree ◯ Hollow Stem/Reed ◯ Crevice/Edge
◯ Other _____

Climate Type: ◯ Dry ◯ Temperate ◯ Tropical ◯ Other_____

Weather Conditions _____

Color: ◯ Black ◯ Yellow ◯ Brown ◯ White ◯ Blue ◯ Red
◯ Orange ◯ Purple ◯ Green ◯ Striped ◯ (Other) _____

Body: ◯ Round/Chubby ◯ Slender ◯ Furry ◯ (Other) _____

Stinger: ◯ Yes ◯ No

Behavior: ◯ Solitary ◯ Brood ◯ Social ◯ Parasitic ◯ Aggressive
◯ (Other) _____

Notes: _____

Wings
Head
Antennae
Thorax
Thorax
Foreleg
Middle Leg
Hindleg

Sketch

---

a.
Similar to drone but have space between eyes.

b.
Similar to worker but have shorter proboscis.

c.
Have huge eyes that touch top of head.

a. Worker / b. Queen / c. Drone
◯ ◯ ◯

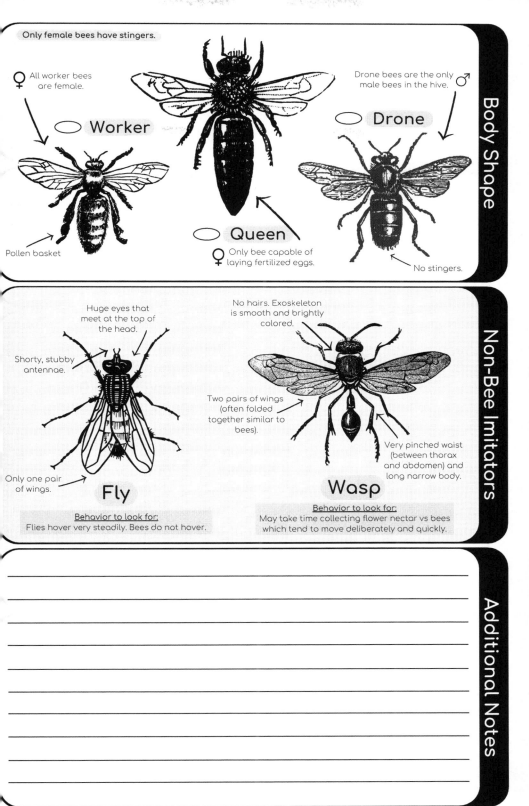

Only female bees have stingers.

♀ All worker bees are female.

Drone bees are the only male bees in the hive. ♂

Worker

Drone

Queen

Pollen basket

♀ Only bee capable of laying fertilized eggs.

No stingers.

Huge eyes that meet at the top of the head.

No hairs. Exoskeleton is smooth and brightly colored.

Shorty, stubby antennae.

Two pairs of wings (often folded together similar to bees).

Very pinched waist (between thorax and abdomen) and long narrow body.

Only one pair of wings.

Fly

Wasp

Behavior to look for:
Flies hover very steadily. Bees do not hover.

Behavior to look for:
May take time collecting flower nectar vs bees which tend to move deliberately and quickly.

Location / GPS: _____ Date _____

Habitat: ◯ Garden ◯ Forest ◯ Woodland ◯ Orchard ◯ Meadow
◯ Other _____

Nest: ◯ Hive ◯ Wood ◯ Tree ◯ Hollow Stem/Reed ◯ Crevice/Edge
◯ Other _____

Climate Type: ◯ Dry ◯ Temperate ◯ Tropical ◯ Other_____

Weather Conditions _____

Color: ◯ Black ◯ Yellow ◯ Brown ◯ White ◯ Blue ◯ Red
◯ Orange ◯ Purple ◯ Green ◯ Striped ◯ (Other) _____

Body: ◯ Round/Chubby ◯ Slender ◯ Furry ◯ (Other) _____

Stinger: ◯ Yes ◯ No

Behavior: ◯ Solitary ◯ Brood ◯ Social ◯ Parasitic ◯ Aggressive
◯ (Other) _____

Notes: _____

Wings — Head
Antennae
Thorax
Thorax
Foreleg
Middle Leg
Hindleg

Sketch

a. Similar to drone but have space between eyes.

b. Similar to worker but have shorter proboscis.

c. Have huge eyes that touch top of head.

a. Worker / b. Queen / c. Drone
◯ ◯ ◯

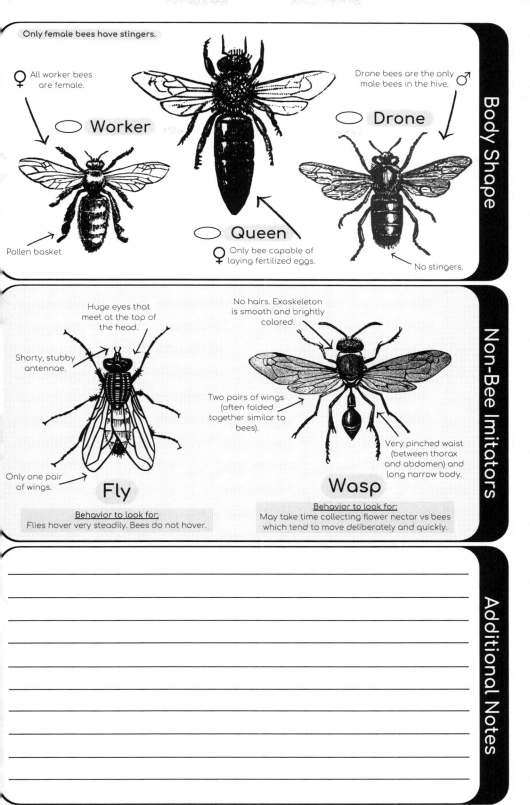

Only female bees have stingers.

All worker bees are female. ♀

Drone bees are the only male bees in the hive. ♂

⬭ Worker

⬭ Drone

⬭ Queen

Only bee capable of laying fertilized eggs. ♀

Pollen basket

No stingers.

Huge eyes that meet at the top of the head.

Shorty, stubby antennae.

Only one pair of wings.

Fly

No hairs. Exoskeleton is smooth and brightly colored.

Two pairs of wings (often folded together similar to bees).

Very pinched waist (between thorax and abdomen) and long narrow body.

Wasp

Behavior to look for:
Flies hover very steadily. Bees do not hover.

Behavior to look for:
May take time collecting flower nectar vs bees which tend to move deliberately and quickly.

_____
_____
_____
_____
_____
_____
_____
_____
_____
_____
_____

Location / GPS: _____ Date _____

Habitat: ◯ Garden ◯ Forest ◯ Woodland ◯ Orchard ◯ Meadow
◯ Other _____

Nest: ◯ Hive ◯ Wood ◯ Tree ◯ Hollow Stem/Reed ◯ Crevice/Edge
◯ Other _____

Climate Type: ◯ Dry ◯ Temperate ◯ Tropical ◯ Other_____

Weather Conditions _____

General

Color: ◯ Black ◯ Yellow ◯ Brown ◯ White ◯ Blue ◯ Red
◯ Orange ◯ Purple ◯ Green ◯ Striped ◯ (Other) _____

Body: ◯ Round/Chubby ◯ Slender ◯ Furry ◯ (Other) _____

Stinger: ◯ Yes ◯ No

Behavior: ◯ Solitary ◯ Brood ◯ Social ◯ Parasitic ◯ Aggressive
◯ (Other) _____

Notes: _____

Characteristics

Wings
Head
Antennae
Thorax
Thorax
Foreleg
Middle Leg
Hindleg

Sketch

Head Shape

a. Similar to drone but have space between eyes.

b. Similar to worker but have shorter proboscis.

c. Have huge eyes that touch top of head.

a. <u>Worker</u> / b. <u>Queen</u> / c. <u>Drone</u>
◯ ◯ ◯

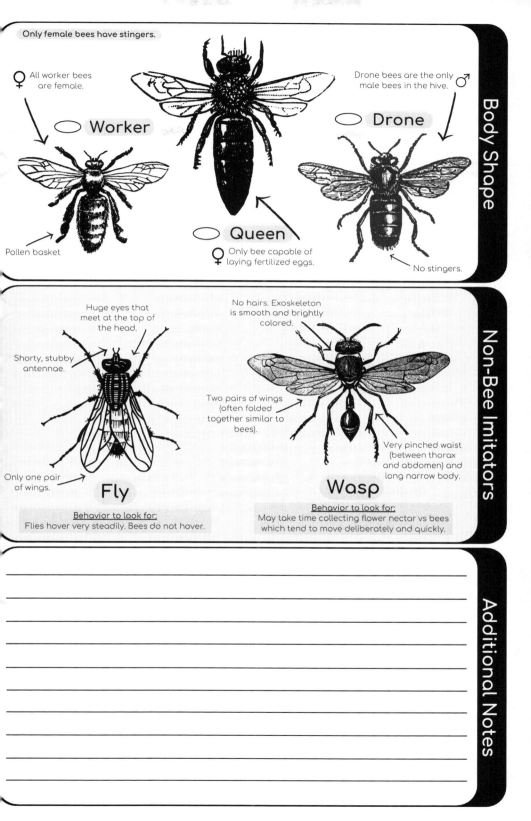

Only female bees have stingers.

All worker bees are female. ♀

Worker

Drone bees are the only ♂ male bees in the hive.

Drone

Pollen basket

Queen

Only bee capable of ♀ laying fertilized eggs.

No stingers.

Huge eyes that meet at the top of the head.

No hairs. Exoskeleton is smooth and brightly colored.

Shorty, stubby antennae.

Two pairs of wings (often folded together similar to bees).

Very pinched waist (between thorax and abdomen) and long narrow body.

Only one pair of wings.

Fly

Behavior to look for:
Flies hover very steadily. Bees do not hover.

Wasp

Behavior to look for:
May take time collecting flower nectar vs bees which tend to move deliberately and quickly.

Location / GPS: _____ Date _____

Habitat: ◯ Garden ◯ Forest ◯ Woodland ◯ Orchard ◯ Meadow
◯ Other _____

Nest: ◯ Hive ◯ Wood ◯ Tree ◯ Hollow Stem/Reed ◯ Crevice/Edge
◯ Other _____

Climate Type: ◯ Dry ◯ Temperate ◯ Tropical ◯ Other_____

Weather Conditions _____

Color: ◯ Black ◯ Yellow ◯ Brown ◯ White ◯ Blue ◯ Red
◯ Orange ◯ Purple ◯ Green ◯ Striped ◯ (Other) _____

Body: ◯ Round/Chubby ◯ Slender ◯ Furry ◯ (Other) _____

Stinger: ◯ Yes ◯ No

Behavior: ◯ Solitary ◯ Brood ◯ Social ◯ Parasitic ◯ Aggressive
◯ (Other) _____

Notes: _____

Wings
Head
Antennae
Thorax
Thorax
Foreleg
Middle Leg
Hindleg

Sketch

a.
Similar to drone but have space between eyes.

b.
Similar to worker but have shorter proboscis.

c.
Have huge eyes that touch top of head.

a. **Worker** / b. **Queen** / c. **Drone**
◯   ◯   ◯

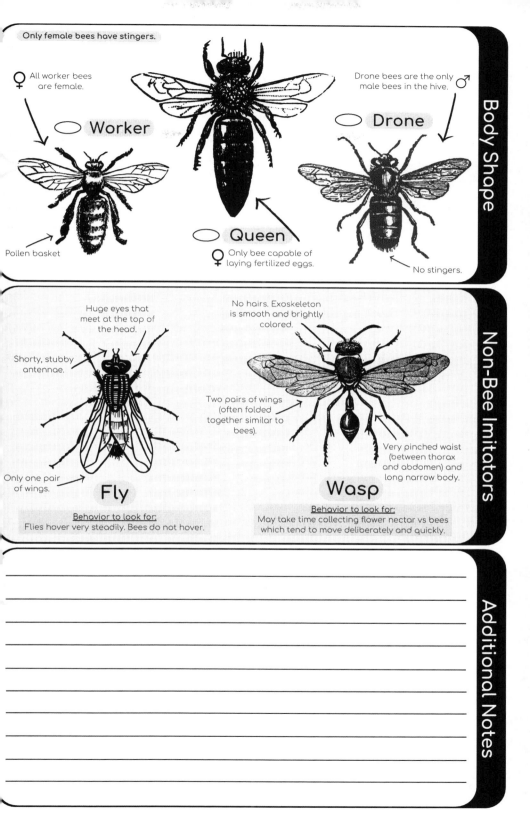

Only female bees have stingers.

Body Shape

All worker bees are female.

Worker

Drone bees are the only male bees in the hive.

Drone

Queen

Only bee capable of laying fertilized eggs.

Pollen basket

No stingers.

Non-Bee Imitators

Huge eyes that meet at the top of the head.

Shorty, stubby antennae.

No hairs. Exoskeleton is smooth and brightly colored.

Two pairs of wings (often folded together similar to bees).

Only one pair of wings.

Fly

Very pinched waist (between thorax and abdomen) and long narrow body.

Wasp

Behavior to look for:
Flies hover very steadily. Bees do not hover.

Behavior to look for:
May take time collecting flower nectar vs bees which tend to move deliberately and quickly.

Additional Notes

Environment

Location / GPS: _____ Date _____

Habitat: ◯ Garden ◯ Forest ◯ Woodland ◯ Orchard ◯ Meadow
         ◯ Other _____

Nest: ◯ Hive ◯ Wood ◯ Tree ◯ Hollow Stem/Reed ◯ Crevice/Edge
      ◯ Other _____

Climate Type: ◯ Dry ◯ Temperate ◯ Tropical ◯ Other _____

Weather Conditions _____

General

Color: ◯ Black ◯ Yellow ◯ Brown ◯ White ◯ Blue ◯ Red
       ◯ Orange ◯ Purple ◯ Green ◯ Striped ◯ (Other) _____

Body: ◯ Round/Chubby ◯ Slender ◯ Furry ◯ (Other) _____

Stinger: ◯ Yes ◯ No

Behavior: ◯ Solitary ◯ Brood ◯ Social ◯ Parasitic ◯ Aggressive
          ◯ (Other) _____

Notes: _____

Characteristics

Wings, Head, Antennae, Thorax, Foreleg, Middle Leg, Hindleg, Thorax

Sketch

Head Shape

a. Similar to drone but have space between eyes.

b. Similar to worker but have shorter proboscis.

c. Have huge eyes that touch top of head.

a. **Worker** / b. **Queen** / c. **Drone**
◯   ◯   ◯

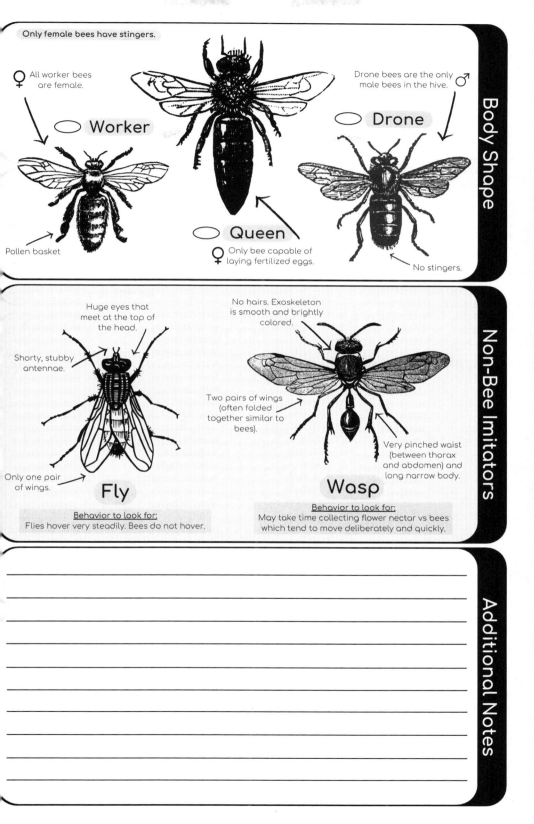

Only female bees have stingers.

♀ All worker bees are female.

Worker

Pollen basket

Queen

♀ Only bee capable of laying fertilized eggs.

Drone bees are the only male bees in the hive. ♂

Drone

No stingers.

Huge eyes that meet at the top of the head.

Shorty, stubby antennae.

Only one pair of wings.

Fly

Behavior to look for:
Flies hover very steadily. Bees do not hover.

No hairs. Exoskeleton is smooth and brightly colored.

Two pairs of wings (often folded together similar to bees).

Very pinched waist (between thorax and abdomen) and long narrow body.

Wasp

Behavior to look for:
May take time collecting flower nectar vs bees which tend to move deliberately and quickly.

Environment

Location / GPS: _____ Date _____

Habitat: ○ Garden ○ Forest ○ Woodland ○ Orchard ○ Meadow
○ Other _____

Nest: ○ Hive ○ Wood ○ Tree ○ Hollow Stem/Reed ○ Crevice/Edge
○ Other _____

Climate Type: ○ Dry ○ Temperate ○ Tropical ○ Other_____

Weather Conditions _____

General

Color: ○ Black ○ Yellow ○ Brown ○ White ○ Blue ○ Red
○ Orange ○ Purple ○ Green ○ Striped ○ (Other) _____

Body: ○ Round/Chubby ○ Slender ○ Furry ○ (Other) _____

Stinger: ○ Yes ○ No

Behavior: ○ Solitary ○ Brood ○ Social ○ Parasitic ○ Aggressive
○ (Other) _____

Notes: _____

Characteristics

Wings
Head
Antennae
Thorax
Foreleg
Thorax
Middle Leg
Hindleg

Sketch

Head Shape

a. Similar to drone but have space between eyes.

b. Similar to worker but have shorter proboscis.

c. Have huge eyes that touch top of head.

a. <u>Worker</u> / b. <u>Queen</u> / c. <u>Drone</u>
○   ○   ○

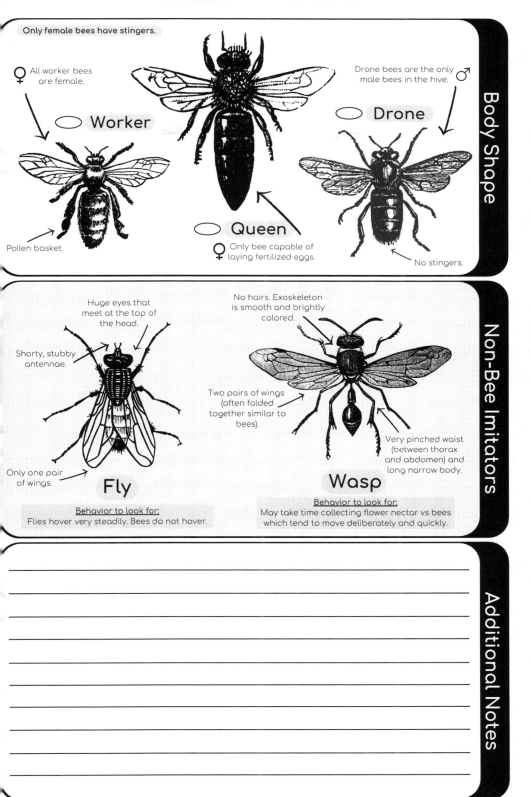

Only female bees have stingers.

♀ All worker bees are female.

Worker

Drone bees are the only male bees in the hive. ♂

Drone

Pollen basket

Queen

♀ Only bee capable of laying fertilized eggs.

No stingers.

Huge eyes that meet at the top of the head.

No hairs. Exoskeleton is smooth and brightly colored.

Shorty, stubby antennae.

Two pairs of wings (often folded together similar to bees).

Only one pair of wings.

Fly

Very pinched waist (between thorax and abdomen) and long narrow body.

Wasp

Behavior to look for:
Flies hover very steadily. Bees do not hover.

Behavior to look for:
May take time collecting flower nectar vs bees which tend to move deliberately and quickly.

Environment

Location / GPS: _____ Date _____

Habitat: ◯ Garden ◯ Forest ◯ Woodland ◯ Orchard ◯ Meadow
◯ Other _____

Nest: ◯ Hive ◯ Wood ◯ Tree ◯ Hollow Stem/Reed ◯ Crevice/Edge
◯ Other _____

Climate Type: ◯ Dry ◯ Temperate ◯ Tropical ◯ Other_____

Weather Conditions _____

General

Color: ◯ Black ◯ Yellow ◯ Brown ◯ White ◯ Blue ◯ Red
◯ Orange ◯ Purple ◯ Green ◯ Striped ◯ (Other) _____

Body: ◯ Round/Chubby ◯ Slender ◯ Furry ◯ (Other) _____

Stinger: ◯ Yes ◯ No

Behavior: ◯ Solitary ◯ Brood ◯ Social ◯ Parasitic ◯ Aggressive
◯ (Other) _____

Notes: _____

Characteristics

Wings
Head
Antennae
Thorax
Thorax
Foreleg
Middle Leg
Hindleg

Sketch

Head Shape

a. Similar to drone but have space between eyes.

b. Similar to worker but have shorter proboscis.

c. Have huge eyes that touch top of head.

a. **Worker** / b. **Queen** / c. **Drone**
◯ ◯ ◯

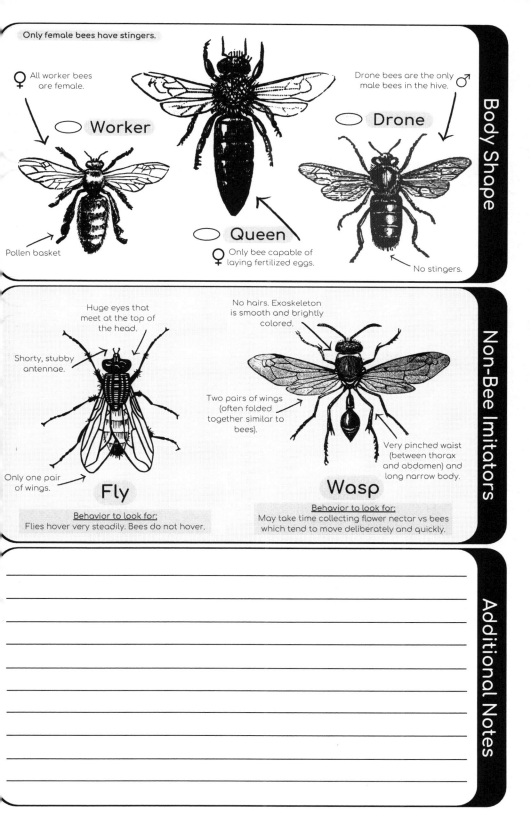

Only female bees have stingers.

All worker bees are female. ♀

Worker

Pollen basket

Queen
♀ Only bee capable of laying fertilized eggs.

Drone bees are the only male bees in the hive. ♂

Drone

No stingers.

Huge eyes that meet at the top of the head.

Shorty, stubby antennae.

Only one pair of wings.

Fly

Behavior to look for:
Flies hover very steadily. Bees do not hover.

No hairs. Exoskeleton is smooth and brightly colored.

Two pairs of wings (often folded together similar to bees).

Very pinched waist (between thorax and abdomen) and long narrow body.

Wasp

Behavior to look for:
May take time collecting flower nectar vs bees which tend to move deliberately and quickly.

Location / GPS: _____   Date _____

Habitat: ◯ Garden ◯ Forest ◯ Woodland ◯ Orchard ◯ Meadow
◯ Other _____

Nest: ◯ Hive ◯ Wood ◯ Tree ◯ Hollow Stem/Reed ◯ Crevice/Edge
◯ Other _____

Climate Type: ◯ Dry ◯ Temperate ◯ Tropical ◯ Other_____

Weather Conditions _____

Color: ◯ Black ◯ Yellow ◯ Brown ◯ White ◯ Blue ◯ Red
◯ Orange ◯ Purple ◯ Green ◯ Striped ◯ (Other) _____

Body: ◯ Round/Chubby ◯ Slender ◯ Furry ◯ (Other) _____

Stinger: ◯ Yes ◯ No

Behavior: ◯ Solitary ◯ Brood ◯ Social ◯ Parasitic ◯ Aggressive
◯ (Other) _____

Notes: _____

Wings → Head Antennae Thorax Foreleg Middle Leg Hindleg Thorax →

Sketch

a. Similar to drone but have space between eyes.

b. Similar to worker but have shorter proboscis.

c. Have huge eyes that touch top of head.

a. Worker / b. Queen / c. Drone
◯   ◯   ◯

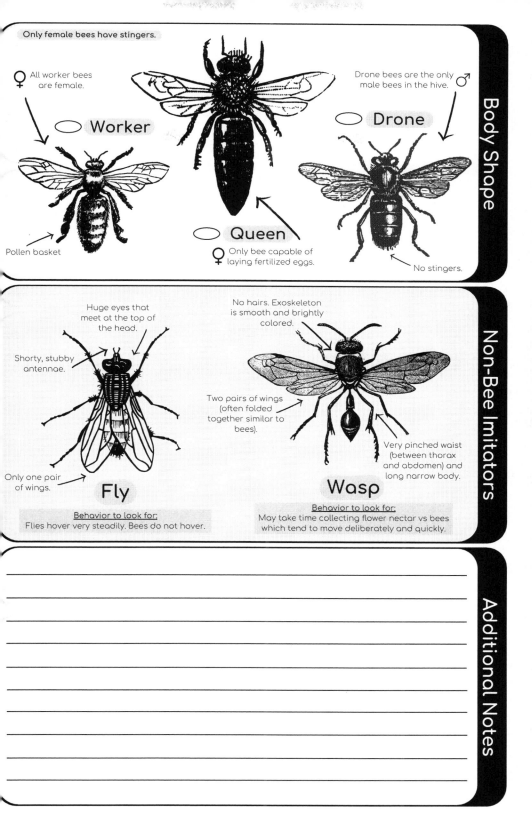

Only female bees have stingers.

All worker bees are female. ♀

Worker

Drone bees are the only male bees in the hive. ♂

Drone

Pollen basket

Queen

Only bee capable of laying fertilized eggs. ♀

No stingers.

Huge eyes that meet at the top of the head.

No hairs. Exoskeleton is smooth and brightly colored.

Shorty, stubby antennae.

Two pairs of wings (often folded together similar to bees).

Very pinched waist (between thorax and abdomen) and long narrow body.

Only one pair of wings.

Fly

Wasp

Behavior to look for:
Flies hover very steadily. Bees do not hover.

Behavior to look for:
May take time collecting flower nectar vs bees which tend to move deliberately and quickly.

Location / GPS: _____ Date _____

Habitat: ◯ Garden ◯ Forest ◯ Woodland ◯ Orchard ◯ Meadow
◯ Other _____

Nest: ◯ Hive ◯ Wood ◯ Tree ◯ Hollow Stem/Reed ◯ Crevice/Edge
◯ Other _____

Climate Type: ◯ Dry ◯ Temperate ◯ Tropical ◯ Other_____

Weather Conditions _____

General

Color: ◯ Black ◯ Yellow ◯ Brown ◯ White ◯ Blue ◯ Red
◯ Orange ◯ Purple ◯ Green ◯ Striped ◯(Other) _____

Body: ◯ Round/Chubby ◯ Slender ◯ Furry ◯(Other) _____

Stinger: ◯ Yes ◯ No

Behavior: ◯ Solitary ◯ Brood ◯ Social ◯ Parasitic ◯ Aggressive
◯(Other) _____

Notes: _____

Characteristics

Wings → Head
Antennae
Thorax
Thorax →
Foreleg
Middle Leg
Hindleg

Sketch

Head Shape

a. Similar to drone but have space between eyes.

b. Similar to worker but have shorter proboscis.

c. Have huge eyes that touch top of head.

a. **Worker** / b. **Queen** / c. **Drone**
◯   ◯   ◯

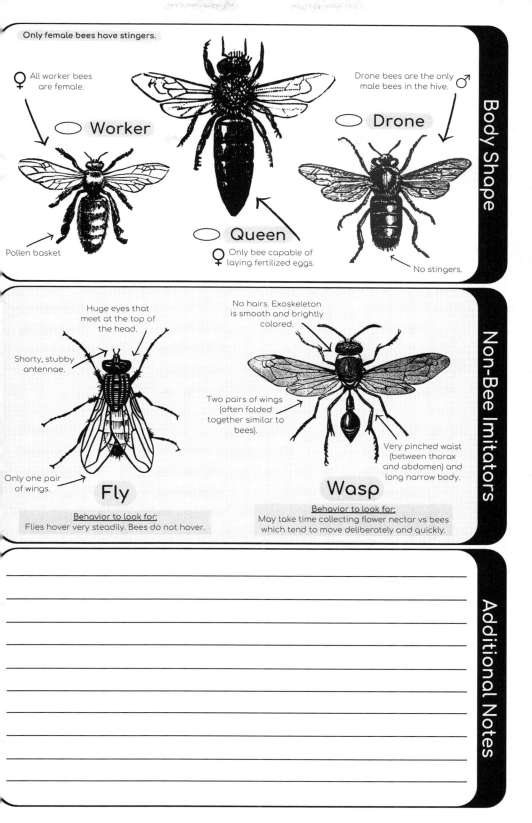

Only female bees have stingers.

♀ All worker bees are female.

Worker

Pollen basket

Queen

♀ Only bee capable of laying fertilized eggs.

Drone bees are the only ♂ male bees in the hive.

Drone

No stingers.

Body Shape

Huge eyes that meet at the top of the head.

Shorty, stubby antennae.

Only one pair of wings.

Fly

Behavior to look for:
Flies hover very steadily. Bees do not hover.

No hairs. Exoskeleton is smooth and brightly colored.

Two pairs of wings (often folded together similar to bees).

Very pinched waist (between thorax and abdomen) and long narrow body.

Wasp

Behavior to look for:
May take time collecting flower nectar vs bees which tend to move deliberately and quickly.

Non-Bee Imitators

Additional Notes

Environment

Location / GPS: _____ Date _____

Habitat: ○ Garden ○ Forest ○ Woodland ○ Orchard ○ Meadow
○ Other _____

Nest: ○ Hive ○ Wood ○ Tree ○ Hollow Stem/Reed ○ Crevice/Edge
○ Other _____

Climate Type: ○ Dry ○ Temperate ○ Tropical ○ Other _____
Weather Conditions _____

General

Color: ○ Black ○ Yellow ○ Brown ○ White ○ Blue ○ Red
○ Orange ○ Purple ○ Green ○ Striped ○ (Other) _____

Body: ○ Round/Chubby ○ Slender ○ Furry ○ (Other) _____

Stinger: ○ Yes ○ No

Behavior: ○ Solitary ○ Brood ○ Social ○ Parasitic ○ Aggressive
○ (Other) _____

Notes: _____

Characteristics

Wings, Head, Antennae, Thorax, Foreleg, Middle Leg, Hindleg, Thorax

Sketch

Head Shape

a. Similar to drone but have space between eyes.
b. Similar to worker but have shorter proboscis.
c. Have huge eyes that touch top of head.

a. **Worker** / b. **Queen** / c. **Drone**
○ ○ ○

Only female bees have stingers.

♀ All worker bees are female.

Drone bees are the only male bees in the hive. ♂

Worker

Drone

Pollen basket

Queen

♀ Only bee capable of laying fertilized eggs.

No stingers.

Huge eyes that meet at the top of the head.

No hairs. Exoskeleton is smooth and brightly colored.

Shorty, stubby antennae.

Two pairs of wings (often folded together similar to bees).

Very pinched waist (between thorax and abdomen) and long narrow body.

Only one pair of wings.

Fly

Wasp

Behavior to look for:
Flies hover very steadily. Bees do not hover.

Behavior to look for:
May take time collecting flower nectar vs bees which tend to move deliberately and quickly.

Environment

Location / GPS: _____ Date _____

Habitat: ○ Garden ○ Forest ○ Woodland ○ Orchard ○ Meadow
○ Other _____

Nest: ○ Hive ○ Wood ○ Tree ○ Hollow Stem/Reed ○ Crevice/Edge
○ Other _____

Climate Type: ○ Dry ○ Temperate ○ Tropical ○ Other_____

Weather Conditions _____

General

Color: ○ Black ○ Yellow ○ Brown ○ White ○ Blue ○ Red
○ Orange ○ Purple ○ Green ○ Striped ○ (Other) _____

Body: ○ Round/Chubby ○ Slender ○ Furry ○ (Other) _____

Stinger: ○ Yes ○ No

Behavior: ○ Solitary ○ Brood ○ Social ○ Parasitic ○ Aggressive
○ (Other) _____

Notes: _____

Characteristics

Wings, Head, Antennae, Thorax, Foreleg, Middle Leg, Hindleg, Thorax

Sketch

Head Shape

a. Similar to drone but have space between eyes.

b. Similar to worker but have shorter proboscis.

c. Have huge eyes that touch top of head.

a. Worker / b. Queen / c. Drone
○   ○   ○

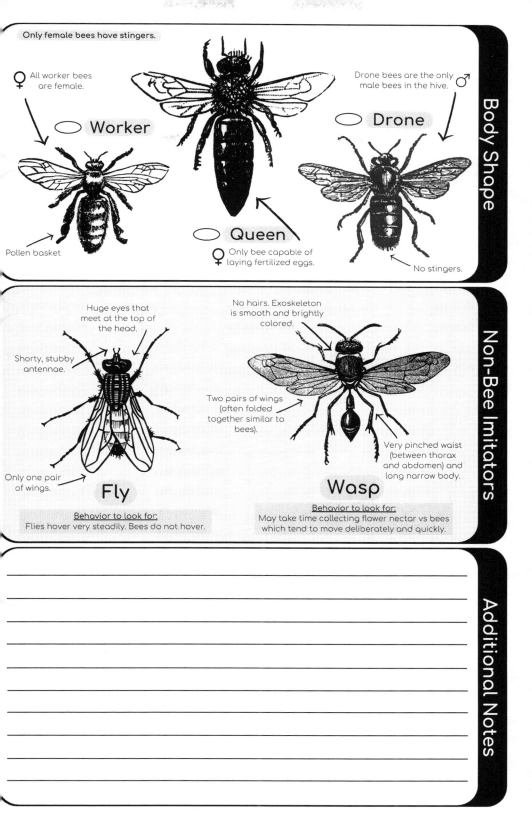

Only female bees have stingers.

♀ All worker bees are female.

○ **Worker**

Pollen basket

○ **Queen**

♀ Only bee capable of laying fertilized eggs.

Drone bees are the only male bees in the hive. ♂

○ **Drone**

No stingers.

Huge eyes that meet at the top of the head.

Shorty, stubby antennae.

Only one pair of wings.

Fly

Behavior to look for:
Flies hover very steadily. Bees do not hover.

No hairs. Exoskeleton is smooth and brightly colored.

Two pairs of wings (often folded together similar to bees).

Very pinched waist (between thorax and abdomen) and long narrow body.

Wasp

Behavior to look for:
May take time collecting flower nectar vs bees which tend to move deliberately and quickly.

Location / GPS: _____ Date _____

Habitat: ◯ Garden ◯ Forest ◯ Woodland ◯ Orchard ◯ Meadow
◯ Other _____

Nest: ◯ Hive ◯ Wood ◯ Tree ◯ Hollow Stem/Reed ◯ Crevice/Edge
◯ Other _____

Climate Type: ◯ Dry ◯ Temperate ◯ Tropical ◯ Other _____

Weather Conditions _____

Color: ◯ Black ◯ Yellow ◯ Brown ◯ White ◯ Blue ◯ Red
◯ Orange ◯ Purple ◯ Green ◯ Striped ◯ (Other) _____

Body: ◯ Round/Chubby ◯ Slender ◯ Furry ◯ (Other) _____

Stinger: ◯ Yes ◯ No

Behavior: ◯ Solitary ◯ Brood ◯ Social ◯ Parasitic ◯ Aggressive
◯ (Other) _____

Notes: _____

Wings →
Head
Antennae
Thorax
Foreleg
Middle Leg
Hindleg
Thorax →

Sketch

a.
Similar to drone but have space between eyes.

b.
Similar to worker but have shorter proboscis.

c.
Have huge eyes that touch top of head.

a. **Worker** / b. **Queen** / c. **Drone**
◯ ◯ ◯

Only female bees have stingers.

♀ All worker bees are female.

Worker

Drone bees are the only male bees in the hive. ♂

Drone

Pollen basket

Queen

♀ Only bee capable of laying fertilized eggs.

No stingers.

Huge eyes that meet at the top of the head.

No hairs. Exoskeleton is smooth and brightly colored.

Shorty, stubby antennae.

Two pairs of wings (often folded together similar to bees).

Very pinched waist (between thorax and abdomen) and long narrow body.

Only one pair of wings.

Fly

Wasp

Behavior to look for:
Flies hover very steadily. Bees do not hover.

Behavior to look for:
May take time collecting flower nectar vs bees which tend to move deliberately and quickly.

Location / GPS: _____ Date _____

Habitat: ◯ Garden ◯ Forest ◯ Woodland ◯ Orchard ◯ Meadow
◯ Other _____

Nest: ◯ Hive ◯ Wood ◯ Tree ◯ Hollow Stem/Reed ◯ Crevice/Edge
◯ Other _____

Climate Type: ◯ Dry ◯ Temperate ◯ Tropical ◯ Other _____

Weather Conditions _____

Color: ◯ Black ◯ Yellow ◯ Brown ◯ White ◯ Blue ◯ Red
◯ Orange ◯ Purple ◯ Green ◯ Striped ◯ (Other) _____

Body: ◯ Round/Chubby ◯ Slender ◯ Furry ◯ (Other) _____

Stinger: ◯ Yes ◯ No

Behavior: ◯ Solitary ◯ Brood ◯ Social ◯ Parasitic ◯ Aggressive
◯ (Other) _____

Notes: _____

Wings →

Head

Antennae

Thorax

Thorax →

Foreleg

Middle Leg

Hindleg

Sketch

a.

Similar to drone but have space between eyes.

b.

Similar to worker but have shorter proboscis.

c.

Have huge eyes that touch top of head.

a. Worker / b. Queen / c. Drone
◯ ◯ ◯

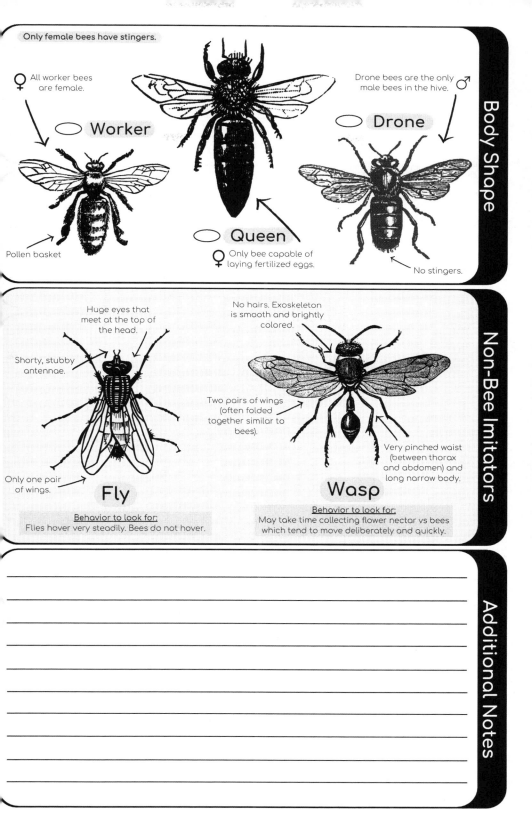

Only female bees have stingers.

♀ All worker bees are female.

◯ Worker

Pollen basket

◯ Queen

♀ Only bee capable of laying fertilized eggs.

Drone bees are the only male bees in the hive. ♂

◯ Drone

No stingers.

Huge eyes that meet at the top of the head.

Shorty, stubby antennae.

Only one pair of wings.

Fly

Behavior to look for:
Flies hover very steadily. Bees do not hover.

No hairs. Exoskeleton is smooth and brightly colored.

Two pairs of wings (often folded together similar to bees).

Very pinched waist (between thorax and abdomen) and long narrow body.

Wasp

Behavior to look for:
May take time collecting flower nectar vs bees which tend to move deliberately and quickly.

Environment

Location / GPS: _____ Date _____

Habitat: ◯ Garden ◯ Forest ◯ Woodland ◯ Orchard ◯ Meadow
◯ Other _____

Nest: ◯ Hive ◯ Wood ◯ Tree ◯ Hollow Stem/Reed ◯ Crevice/Edge
◯ Other _____

Climate Type: ◯ Dry ◯ Temperate ◯ Tropical ◯ Other_____

Weather Conditions _____

General

Color: ◯ Black ◯ Yellow ◯ Brown ◯ White ◯ Blue ◯ Red
◯ Orange ◯ Purple ◯ Green ◯ Striped ◯ (Other) _____

Body: ◯ Round/Chubby ◯ Slender ◯ Furry ◯ (Other) _____

Stinger: ◯ Yes ◯ No

Behavior: ◯ Solitary ◯ Brood ◯ Social ◯ Parasitic ◯ Aggressive
◯ (Other) _____

Notes: _____

Characteristics

Wings →

Head

Antennae

Thorax

Thorax →

Foreleg

Middle Leg

Hindleg

Sketch

Head Shape

a. Similar to drone but have space between eyes.

b. Similar to worker but have shorter proboscis.

c. Have huge eyes that touch top of head.

a. <u>Worker</u> / b. <u>Queen</u> / c. <u>Drone</u>
◯ ◯ ◯

Only female bees have stingers.

♀ All worker bees are female.

Worker

Pollen basket

Queen

♀ Only bee capable of laying fertilized eggs.

Drone bees are the only male bees in the hive. ♂

Drone

No stingers.

Body Shape

Huge eyes that meet at the top of the head.

Shorty, stubby antennae.

Only one pair of wings.

Fly

Behavior to look for:
Flies hover very steadily. Bees do not hover.

No hairs. Exoskeleton is smooth and brightly colored.

Two pairs of wings (often folded together similar to bees).

Very pinched waist (between thorax and abdomen) and long narrow body.

Wasp

Behavior to look for:
May take time collecting flower nectar vs bees which tend to move deliberately and quickly.

Non-Bee Imitators

Additional Notes

Location / GPS: _____ Date _____

Habitat: ◯ Garden ◯ Forest ◯ Woodland ◯ Orchard ◯ Meadow
◯ Other _____

Nest: ◯ Hive ◯ Wood ◯ Tree ◯ Hollow Stem/Reed ◯ Crevice/Edge
◯ Other _____

Climate Type: ◯ Dry ◯ Temperate ◯ Tropical ◯ Other_____

Weather Conditions _____

Color: ◯ Black ◯ Yellow ◯ Brown ◯ White ◯ Blue ◯ Red
◯ Orange ◯ Purple ◯ Green ◯ Striped ◯ (Other) _____

Body: ◯ Round/Chubby ◯ Slender ◯ Furry ◯ (Other) _____

Stinger: ◯ Yes ◯ No

Behavior: ◯ Solitary ◯ Brood ◯ Social ◯ Parasitic ◯ Aggressive
◯ (Other) _____

Notes: _____

Wings →
Head
Antennae
Thorax
Thorax →
Foreleg
Middle Leg
Hindleg

Sketch

a.
Similar to drone but have space between eyes.

b.
Similar to worker but have shorter proboscis.

c.
Have huge eyes that touch top of head.

a. Worker / b. Queen / c. Drone
◯ ◯ ◯

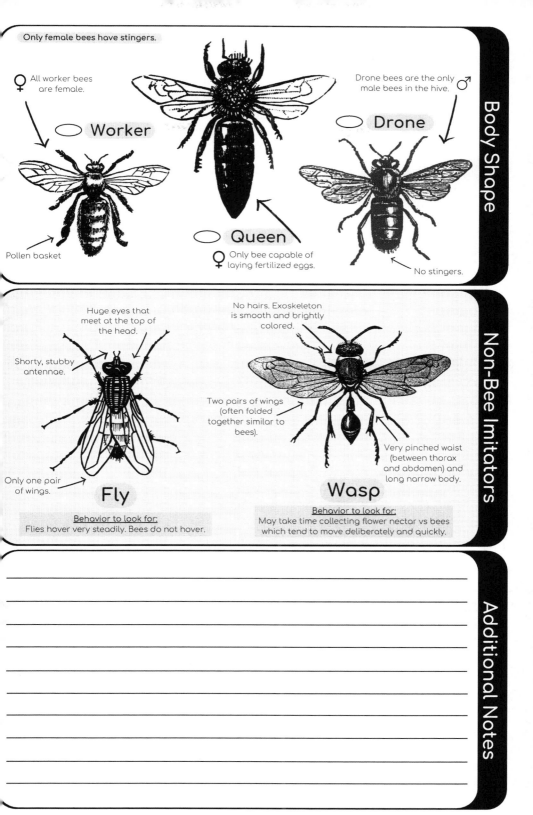

Only female bees have stingers.

♀ All worker bees are female.

Worker

Pollen basket

Drone bees are the only male bees in the hive. ♂

Drone

Queen

♀ Only bee capable of laying fertilized eggs.

No stingers.

Huge eyes that meet at the top of the head.

Shorty, stubby antennae.

No hairs. Exoskeleton is smooth and brightly colored.

Two pairs of wings (often folded together similar to bees).

Very pinched waist (between thorax and abdomen) and long narrow body.

Only one pair of wings.

Fly

Behavior to look for:
Flies hover very steadily. Bees do not hover.

Wasp

Behavior to look for:
May take time collecting flower nectar vs bees which tend to move deliberately and quickly.

Location / GPS: _____ Date _____

Habitat: ◯ Garden ◯ Forest ◯ Woodland ◯ Orchard ◯ Meadow
         ◯ Other _____

Nest: ◯ Hive ◯ Wood ◯ Tree ◯ Hollow Stem/Reed ◯ Crevice/Edge
      ◯ Other _____

Climate Type: ◯ Dry ◯ Temperate ◯ Tropical ◯ Other_____

Weather Conditions _____

General

Color: ◯ Black ◯ Yellow ◯ Brown ◯ White ◯ Blue ◯ Red
       ◯ Orange ◯ Purple ◯ Green ◯ Striped ◯ (Other) _____

Body: ◯ Round/Chubby ◯ Slender ◯ Furry ◯ (Other) _____

Stinger: ◯ Yes ◯ No

Behavior: ◯ Solitary ◯ Brood ◯ Social ◯ Parasitic ◯ Aggressive
          ◯ (Other) _____

Notes: _____

Characteristics

Wings

Head

Antennae

Thorax

Thorax

Foreleg

Middle Leg

Hindleg

Sketch

Head Shape

a.
Similar to drone but have space between eyes.

b.

c.
Have huge eyes that touch top of head.

Similar to worker but have shorter proboscis.

a. Worker / b. Queen / c. Drone
   ◯   ◯   ◯

Only female bees have stingers.

All worker bees are female. ♀

Worker

Pollen basket

Queen

♀ Only bee capable of laying fertilized eggs.

Drone bees are the only ♂ male bees in the hive.

Drone

No stingers.

Huge eyes that meet at the top of the head.

Shorty, stubby antennae.

No hairs. Exoskeleton is smooth and brightly colored.

Two pairs of wings (often folded together similar to bees).

Only one pair of wings.

Fly

Behavior to look for:
Flies hover very steadily. Bees do not hover.

Very pinched waist (between thorax and abdomen) and long narrow body.

Wasp

Behavior to look for:
May take time collecting flower nectar vs bees which tend to move deliberately and quickly.

Location / GPS: _____ Date _____

Habitat: ⭘ Garden ⭘ Forest ⭘ Woodland ⭘ Orchard ⭘ Meadow
⭘ Other _____

Nest: ⭘ Hive ⭘ Wood ⭘ Tree ⭘ Hollow Stem/Reed ⭘ Crevice/Edge
⭘ Other _____

Climate Type: ⭘ Dry ⭘ Temperate ⭘ Tropical ⭘ Other_____

Weather Conditions _____

Color: ⭘ Black ⭘ Yellow ⭘ Brown ⭘ White ⭘ Blue ⭘ Red
⭘ Orange ⭘ Purple ⭘ Green ⭘ Striped ⭘(Other) _____

Body: ⭘ Round/Chubby ⭘ Slender ⭘ Furry ⭘(Other) _____

Stinger: ⭘ Yes ⭘ No

Behavior: ⭘ Solitary ⭘ Brood ⭘ Social ⭘ Parasitic ⭘ Aggressive
⭘(Other) _____

Notes: _____

Wings — Head

Antennae

Thorax

Thorax

Foreleg

Middle Leg

Hindleg

Sketch

a.

Similar to drone but have space between eyes.

b.

c.

Similar to worker but have shorter proboscis.

Have huge eyes that touch top of head.

a. **Worker** / b. **Queen** / c. **Drone**
⭘ ⭘ ⭘

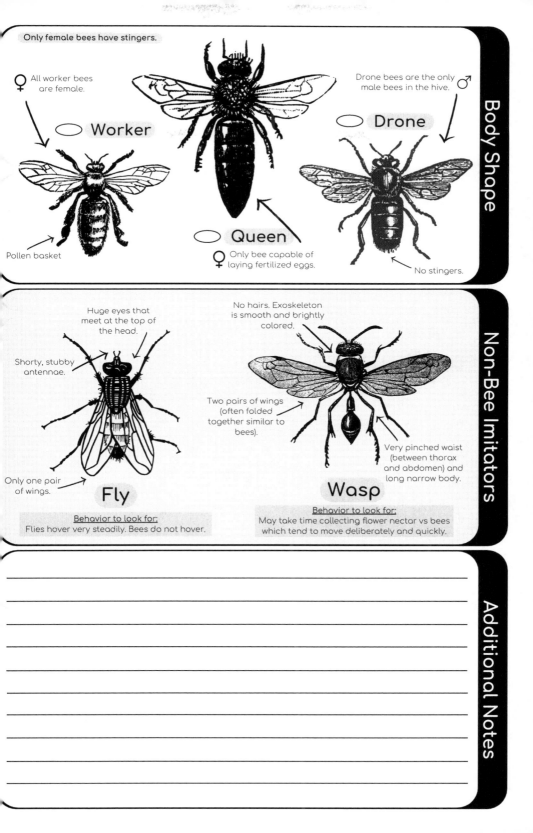

Only female bees have stingers.

All worker bees are female. ♀

Drone bees are the only male bees in the hive. ♂

Worker

Drone

Pollen basket

Queen

♀ Only bee capable of laying fertilized eggs.

No stingers.

Huge eyes that meet at the top of the head.

No hairs. Exoskeleton is smooth and brightly colored.

Shorty, stubby antennae.

Two pairs of wings (often folded together similar to bees).

Very pinched waist (between thorax and abdomen) and long narrow body.

Only one pair of wings.

Fly

Behavior to look for:
Flies hover very steadily. Bees do not hover.

Wasp

Behavior to look for:
May take time collecting flower nectar vs bees which tend to move deliberately and quickly.

Location / GPS: _____ **Date** _____

Habitat: ◯ Garden ◯ Forest ◯ Woodland ◯ Orchard ◯ Meadow
◯ Other _____

Nest: ◯ Hive ◯ Wood ◯ Tree ◯ Hollow Stem/Reed ◯ Crevice/Edge
◯ Other _____

Climate Type: ◯ Dry ◯ Temperate ◯ Tropical ◯ Other_____

Weather Conditions _____

General

Color: ◯ Black ◯ Yellow ◯ Brown ◯ White ◯ Blue ◯ Red
◯ Orange ◯ Purple ◯ Green ◯ Striped ◯ (Other) _____

Body: ◯ Round/Chubby ◯ Slender ◯ Furry ◯ (Other) _____

Stinger: ◯ Yes ◯ No

Behavior: ◯ Solitary ◯ Brood ◯ Social ◯ Parasitic ◯ Aggressive
◯ (Other) _____

Notes: _____

Characteristics

Wings

Head

Antennae

Thorax

Thorax

Foreleg

Middle Leg

Hindleg

Sketch

Head Shape

a.
Similar to drone but have space between eyes.

b.
Similar to worker but have shorter proboscis.

c.
Have huge eyes that touch top of head.

a. <u>Worker</u> / b. <u>Queen</u> / c. <u>Drone</u>
◯   ◯   ◯

Only female bees have stingers.

All worker bees are female. ♀

Drone bees are the only male bees in the hive. ♂

○ Worker

○ Drone

Pollen basket

○ Queen

♀ Only bee capable of laying fertilized eggs.

No stingers.

Huge eyes that meet at the top of the head.

No hairs. Exoskeleton is smooth and brightly colored.

Shorty, stubby antennae.

Two pairs of wings (often folded together similar to bees).

Only one pair of wings.

Fly

Very pinched waist (between thorax and abdomen) and long narrow body.

Wasp

Behavior to look for:
Flies hover very steadily. Bees do not hover.

Behavior to look for:
May take time collecting flower nectar vs bees which tend to move deliberately and quickly.

Location / GPS: _____ Date _____

Habitat: ◯ Garden ◯ Forest ◯ Woodland ◯ Orchard ◯ Meadow
◯ Other _____

Nest: ◯ Hive ◯ Wood ◯ Tree ◯ Hollow Stem/Reed ◯ Crevice/Edge
◯ Other _____

Climate Type: ◯ Dry ◯ Temperate ◯ Tropical ◯ Other_____

Weather Conditions _____

Color: ◯ Black ◯ Yellow ◯ Brown ◯ White ◯ Blue ◯ Red
◯ Orange ◯ Purple ◯ Green ◯ Striped ◯(Other) _____

Body: ◯ Round/Chubby ◯ Slender ◯ Furry ◯(Other) _____

Stinger: ◯ Yes ◯ No

Behavior: ◯ Solitary ◯ Brood ◯ Social ◯ Parasitic ◯ Aggressive
◯(Other) _____

Notes: _____

Wings
Head
Antennae
Thorax
Thorax
Foreleg
Middle Leg
Hindleg

Sketch

a.
Similar to drone but have space between eyes.

b.
Similar to worker but have shorter proboscis.

c.
Have huge eyes that touch top of head.

a. Worker / b. Queen / c. Drone
◯ ◯ ◯

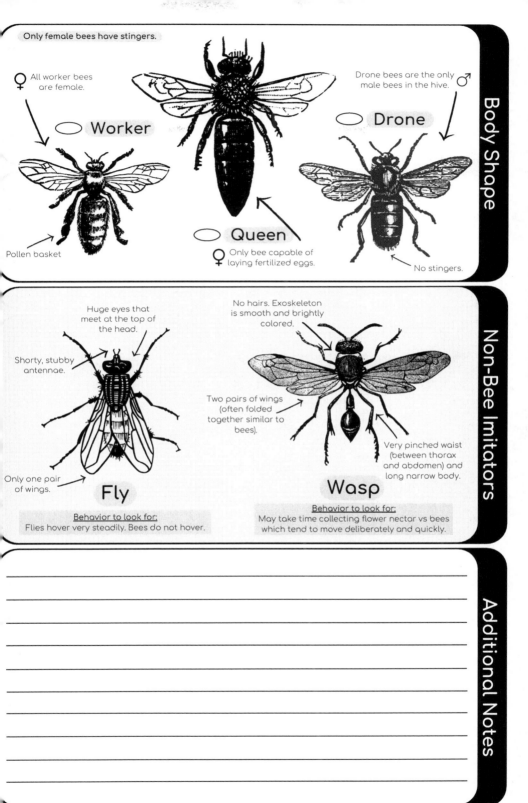

Body Shape

Only female bees have stingers.

♀ All worker bees are female.

◯ Worker

Pollen basket

◯ Queen

♀ Only bee capable of laying fertilized eggs.

♂ Drone bees are the only male bees in the hive.

◯ Drone

No stingers.

Non-Bee Imitators

Huge eyes that meet at the top of the head.

Shorty, stubby antennae.

Only one pair of wings.

Fly

Behavior to look for:
Flies hover very steadily. Bees do not hover.

No hairs. Exoskeleton is smooth and brightly colored.

Two pairs of wings (often folded together similar to bees).

Very pinched waist (between thorax and abdomen) and long narrow body.

Wasp

Behavior to look for:
May take time collecting flower nectar vs bees which tend to move deliberately and quickly.

Additional Notes

Location / GPS: _____ Date _____

Habitat: ◯ Garden ◯ Forest ◯ Woodland ◯ Orchard ◯ Meadow
◯ Other _____

Nest: ◯ Hive ◯ Wood ◯ Tree ◯ Hollow Stem/Reed ◯ Crevice/Edge
◯ Other _____

Climate Type: ◯ Dry ◯ Temperate ◯ Tropical ◯ Other_____

Weather Conditions _____

Color: ◯ Black ◯ Yellow ◯ Brown ◯ White ◯ Blue ◯ Red
◯ Orange ◯ Purple ◯ Green ◯ Striped ◯ (Other) _____

Body: ◯ Round/Chubby ◯ Slender ◯ Furry ◯ (Other) _____

Stinger: ◯ Yes ◯ No

Behavior: ◯ Solitary ◯ Brood ◯ Social ◯ Parasitic ◯ Aggressive
◯ (Other) _____

Notes: _____

Wings →

Head

Antennae

Thorax

Thorax →

Foreleg

Middle Leg

Hindleg

Sketch

a.
Similar to drone but have space between eyes.

b.
Similar to worker but have shorter proboscis.

c.
Have huge eyes that touch top of head.

a. Worker / b. Queen / c. Drone
◯   ◯   ◯

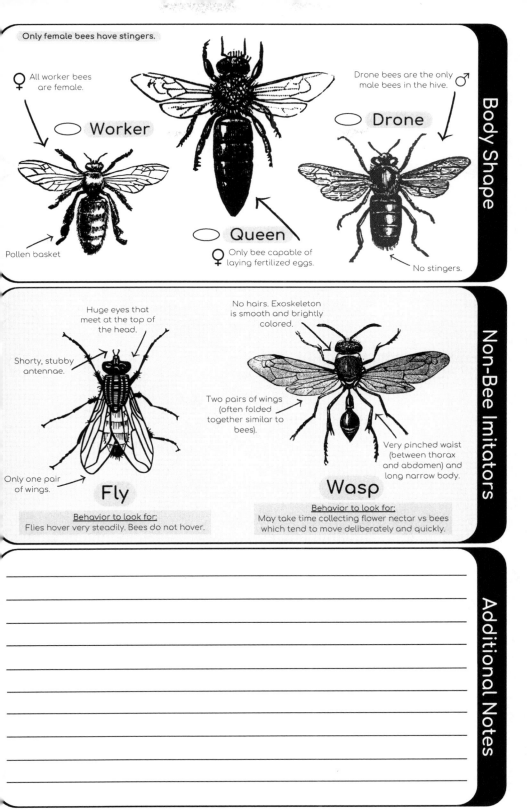

Only female bees have stingers.

♀ All worker bees are female.

Worker

Pollen basket

Queen

♀ Only bee capable of laying fertilized eggs.

Drone bees are the only male bees in the hive. ♂

Drone

No stingers.

Huge eyes that meet at the top of the head.

Shorty, stubby antennae.

Only one pair of wings.

Fly

Behavior to look for:
Flies hover very steadily. Bees do not hover.

No hairs. Exoskeleton is smooth and brightly colored.

Two pairs of wings (often folded together similar to bees).

Very pinched waist (between thorax and abdomen) and long narrow body.

Wasp

Behavior to look for:
May take time collecting flower nectar vs bees which tend to move deliberately and quickly.

Location / GPS: _____ Date _____

Habitat: ◯ Garden ◯ Forest ◯ Woodland ◯ Orchard ◯ Meadow
◯ Other _____

Nest: ◯ Hive ◯ Wood ◯ Tree ◯ Hollow Stem/Reed ◯ Crevice/Edge
◯ Other _____

Climate Type: ◯ Dry ◯ Temperate ◯ Tropical ◯ Other_____

Weather Conditions _____

Color: ◯ Black ◯ Yellow ◯ Brown ◯ White ◯ Blue ◯ Red
◯ Orange ◯ Purple ◯ Green ◯ Striped ◯ (Other) _____

Body: ◯ Round/Chubby ◯ Slender ◯ Furry ◯ (Other) _____

Stinger: ◯ Yes ◯ No

Behavior: ◯ Solitary ◯ Brood ◯ Social ◯ Parasitic ◯ Aggressive
◯ (Other) _____

Notes: _____

Wings → Head
Antennae
Thorax
Thorax → Foreleg
Middle Leg
Hindleg

Sketch

a. Similar to drone but have space between eyes.

b.

c. Have huge eyes that touch top of head.

Similar to worker but have shorter proboscis.

a. Worker / b. Queen / c. Drone
◯   ◯   ◯

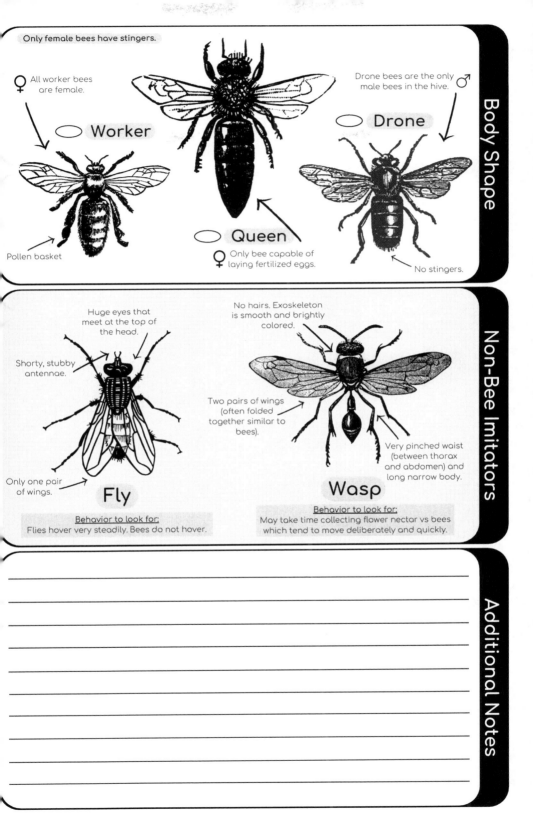

Only female bees have stingers.

♀ All worker bees are female.

Worker

Drone bees are the only male bees in the hive. ♂

Drone

Pollen basket

Queen

♀ Only bee capable of laying fertilized eggs.

No stingers.

Huge eyes that meet at the top of the head.

No hairs. Exoskeleton is smooth and brightly colored.

Shorty, stubby antennae.

Two pairs of wings (often folded together similar to bees).

Only one pair of wings.

Fly

Behavior to look for:
Flies hover very steadily. Bees do not hover.

Very pinched waist (between thorax and abdomen) and long narrow body.

Wasp

Behavior to look for:
May take time collecting flower nectar vs bees which tend to move deliberately and quickly.

Location / GPS: _____ Date _____

Habitat: ◯ Garden ◯ Forest ◯ Woodland ◯ Orchard ◯ Meadow
◯ Other _____

Nest: ◯ Hive ◯ Wood ◯ Tree ◯ Hollow Stem/Reed ◯ Crevice/Edge
◯ Other _____

Climate Type: ◯ Dry ◯ Temperate ◯ Tropical ◯ Other_____

Weather Conditions _____

Color: ◯ Black ◯ Yellow ◯ Brown ◯ White ◯ Blue ◯ Red
◯ Orange ◯ Purple ◯ Green ◯ Striped ◯ (Other) _____

Body: ◯ Round/Chubby ◯ Slender ◯ Furry ◯ (Other) _____

Stinger: ◯ Yes ◯ No

Behavior: ◯ Solitary ◯ Brood ◯ Social ◯ Parasitic ◯ Aggressive
◯ (Other) _____

Notes: _____

Wings
Head
Antennae
Thorax
Thorax
Foreleg
Middle Leg
Hindleg

Sketch

a.
Similar to drone but have space between eyes.

b.
Similar to worker but have shorter proboscis.

c.
Have huge eyes that touch top of head.

a. Worker / b. Queen / c. Drone
◯   ◯   ◯

Only female bees have stingers.

♀ All worker bees are female.

Worker

Pollen basket

Queen

♀ Only bee capable of laying fertilized eggs.

Drone bees are the only male bees in the hive. ♂

Drone

No stingers.

Huge eyes that meet at the top of the head.

Shorty, stubby antennae.

Only one pair of wings.

Fly

Behavior to look for:
Flies hover very steadily. Bees do not hover.

No hairs. Exoskeleton is smooth and brightly colored.

Two pairs of wings (often folded together similar to bees).

Very pinched waist (between thorax and abdomen) and long narrow body.

Wasp

Behavior to look for:
May take time collecting flower nectar vs bees which tend to move deliberately and quickly.

Environment

Location / GPS: _____ Date _____

Habitat: ◯ Garden ◯ Forest ◯ Woodland ◯ Orchard ◯ Meadow
◯ Other _____

Nest: ◯ Hive ◯ Wood ◯ Tree ◯ Hollow Stem/Reed ◯ Crevice/Edge
◯ Other _____

Climate Type: ◯ Dry ◯ Temperate ◯ Tropical ◯ Other_____

Weather Conditions _____

General

Color: ◯ Black ◯ Yellow ◯ Brown ◯ White ◯ Blue ◯ Red
◯ Orange ◯ Purple ◯ Green ◯ Striped ◯(Other) _____

Body: ◯ Round/Chubby ◯ Slender ◯ Furry ◯(Other) _____

Stinger: ◯ Yes ◯ No

Behavior: ◯ Solitary ◯ Brood ◯ Social ◯ Parasitic ◯ Aggressive
◯(Other) _____

Notes: _____

Characteristics

Wings →
Head
Antennae
Thorax
Thorax →
Foreleg
Middle Leg
Hindleg

Sketch

Head Shape

a. Similar to drone but have space between eyes.

b. Similar to worker but have shorter proboscis.

c. Have huge eyes that touch top of head.

a. Worker / b. Queen / c. Drone
◯   ◯   ◯

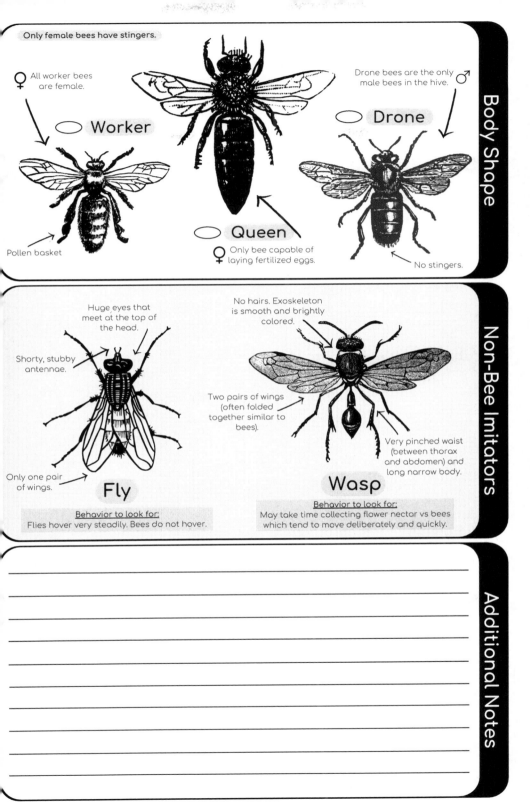

Body Shape

Only female bees have stingers.

♀ All worker bees are female.

○ Worker

Drone bees are the only male bees in the hive. ♂

○ Drone

Pollen basket

○ Queen

♀ Only bee capable of laying fertilized eggs.

No stingers.

Non-Bee Imitators

Huge eyes that meet at the top of the head.

Shorty, stubby antennae.

No hairs. Exoskeleton is smooth and brightly colored.

Two pairs of wings (often folded together similar to bees).

Only one pair of wings.

Fly

Very pinched waist (between thorax and abdomen) and long narrow body.

Wasp

Behavior to look for:
Flies hover very steadily. Bees do not hover.

Behavior to look for:
May take time collecting flower nectar vs bees which tend to move deliberately and quickly.

Additional Notes

Location / GPS: _____ Date _____

Habitat: ◯ Garden ◯ Forest ◯ Woodland ◯ Orchard ◯ Meadow
◯ Other _____

Nest: ◯ Hive ◯ Wood ◯ Tree ◯ Hollow Stem/Reed ◯ Crevice/Edge
◯ Other _____

Climate Type: ◯ Dry ◯ Temperate ◯ Tropical ◯ Other_____

Weather Conditions _____

Color: ◯ Black ◯ Yellow ◯ Brown ◯ White ◯ Blue ◯ Red
◯ Orange ◯ Purple ◯ Green ◯ Striped ◯(Other) _____

Body: ◯ Round/Chubby ◯ Slender ◯ Furry ◯(Other) _____

Stinger: ◯ Yes ◯ No

Behavior: ◯ Solitary ◯ Brood ◯ Social ◯ Parasitic ◯ Aggressive
◯(Other) _____

Notes: _____

Wings →
Head
Antennae
Thorax
Thorax →
Foreleg
Middle Leg
Hindleg

Sketch

a.
Similar to drone but have space between eyes.

b.
Similar to worker but have shorter proboscis.

c.
Have huge eyes that touch top of head.

a. <u>Worker</u> / b. <u>Queen</u> / c. <u>Drone</u>
◯   ◯   ◯

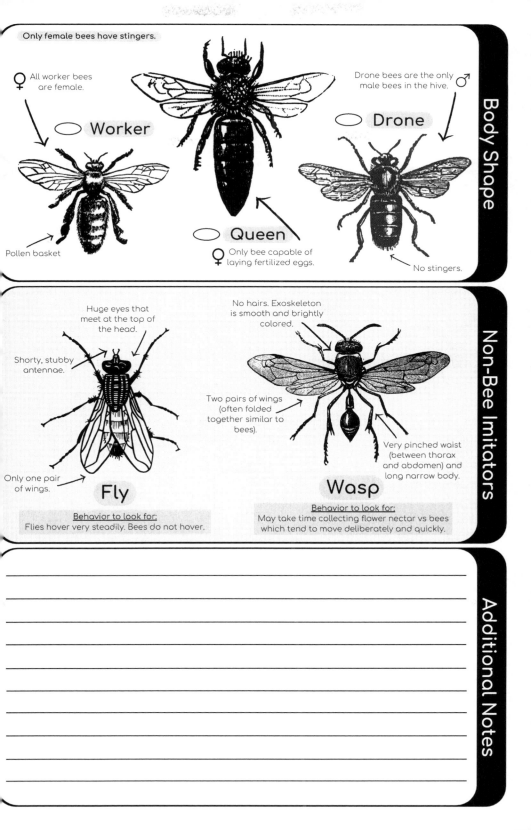

Only female bees have stingers.

All worker bees are female.

Worker

Pollen basket

Queen

Only bee capable of laying fertilized eggs.

Drone bees are the only male bees in the hive.

Drone

No stingers.

Body Shape

Huge eyes that meet at the top of the head.

Shorty, stubby antennae.

Only one pair of wings.

Fly

Behavior to look for:
Flies hover very steadily. Bees do not hover.

No hairs. Exoskeleton is smooth and brightly colored.

Two pairs of wings (often folded together similar to bees).

Very pinched waist (between thorax and abdomen) and long narrow body.

Wasp

Behavior to look for:
May take time collecting flower nectar vs bees which tend to move deliberately and quickly.

Non-Bee Imitators

Additional Notes

Environment

Location / GPS: _____ Date _____

Habitat: ◯ Garden ◯ Forest ◯ Woodland ◯ Orchard ◯ Meadow
◯ Other _____

Nest: ◯ Hive ◯ Wood ◯ Tree ◯ Hollow Stem/Reed ◯ Crevice/Edge
◯ Other _____

Climate Type: ◯ Dry ◯ Temperate ◯ Tropical ◯ Other_____

Weather Conditions _____

General

Color: ◯ Black ◯ Yellow ◯ Brown ◯ White ◯ Blue ◯ Red
◯ Orange ◯ Purple ◯ Green ◯ Striped ◯ (Other) _____

Body: ◯ Round/Chubby ◯ Slender ◯ Furry ◯ (Other) _____

Stinger: ◯ Yes ◯ No

Behavior: ◯ Solitary ◯ Brood ◯ Social ◯ Parasitic ◯ Aggressive
◯ (Other) _____

Notes: _____

Characteristics

Wings — Head — Antennae — Thorax — Foreleg — Middle Leg — Hindleg — Thorax

Sketch

Head Shape

a. Similar to drone but have space between eyes.

b. Similar to worker but have shorter proboscis.

c. Have huge eyes that touch top of head.

a. **Worker** / b. **Queen** / c. **Drone**
◯   ◯   ◯

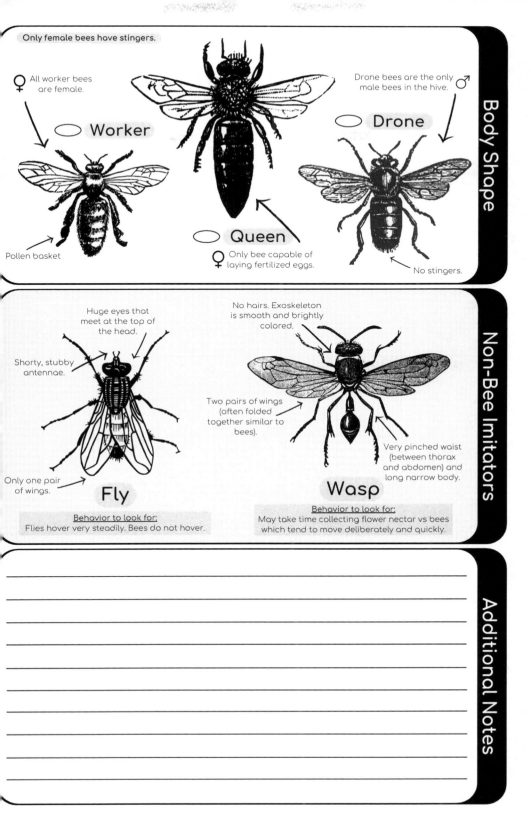

Only female bees have stingers.

♀ All worker bees are female.

◯ **Worker**

Pollen basket

◯ **Queen**

♀ Only bee capable of laying fertilized eggs.

Drone bees are the only male bees in the hive. ♂

◯ **Drone**

No stingers.

Huge eyes that meet at the top of the head.

Shorty, stubby antennae.

Only one pair of wings.

Fly

Behavior to look for:
Flies hover very steadily. Bees do not hover.

No hairs. Exoskeleton is smooth and brightly colored.

Two pairs of wings (often folded together similar to bees).

Very pinched waist (between thorax and abdomen) and long narrow body.

Wasp

Behavior to look for:
May take time collecting flower nectar vs bees which tend to move deliberately and quickly.

Location / GPS: _____ Date _____

Habitat: ◯ Garden ◯ Forest ◯ Woodland ◯ Orchard ◯ Meadow
◯ Other _____

Nest: ◯ Hive ◯ Wood ◯ Tree ◯ Hollow Stem/Reed ◯ Crevice/Edge
◯ Other _____

Climate Type: ◯ Dry ◯ Temperate ◯ Tropical ◯ Other_____

Weather Conditions _____

Color: ◯ Black ◯ Yellow ◯ Brown ◯ White ◯ Blue ◯ Red
◯ Orange ◯ Purple ◯ Green ◯ Striped ◯ (Other) _____

Body: ◯ Round/Chubby ◯ Slender ◯ Furry ◯ (Other) _____

Stinger: ◯ Yes ◯ No

Behavior: ◯ Solitary ◯ Brood ◯ Social ◯ Parasitic ◯ Aggressive
◯ (Other) _____

Notes: _____

Wings → | Head
Antennae
Thorax
Thorax → | Foreleg
Middle Leg
Hindleg

Sketch

a. Similar to drone but have space between eyes.

b. Similar to worker but have shorter proboscis.

c. Have huge eyes that touch top of head.

a. __Worker__ / b. __Queen__ / c. __Drone__
◯   ◯   ◯

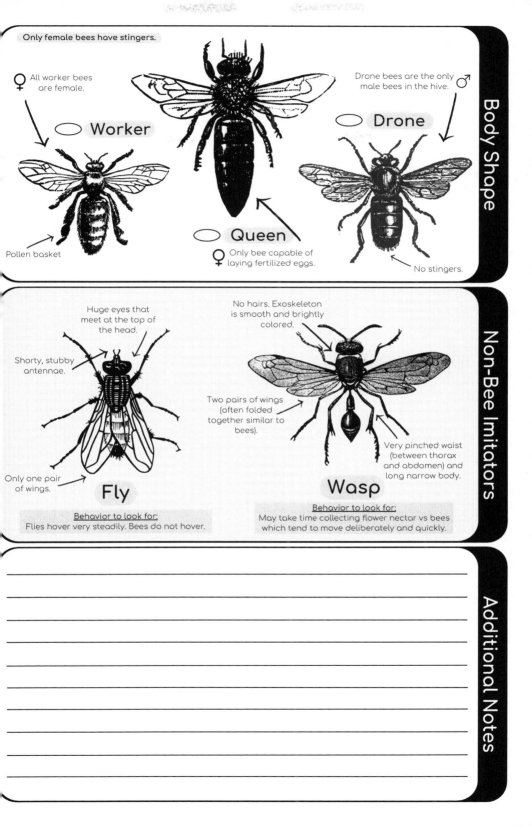

Only female bees have stingers.

All worker bees are female. ♀

Worker

Drone bees are the only male bees in the hive. ♂

Drone

Pollen basket

Queen

♀ Only bee capable of laying fertilized eggs.

No stingers.

Huge eyes that meet at the top of the head.

No hairs. Exoskeleton is smooth and brightly colored.

Shorty, stubby antennae.

Two pairs of wings (often folded together similar to bees).

Only one pair of wings

Fly

Very pinched waist (between thorax and abdomen) and long narrow body.

Wasp

Behavior to look for:
Flies hover very steadily. Bees do not hover.

Behavior to look for:
May take time collecting flower nectar vs bees which tend to move deliberately and quickly.

Location / GPS: _____ **Date** _____

Habitat: ○ Garden ○ Forest ○ Woodland ○ Orchard ○ Meadow
○ Other _____

Nest: ○ Hive ○ Wood ○ Tree ○ Hollow Stem/Reed ○ Crevice/Edge
○ Other _____

Climate Type: ○ Dry ○ Temperate ○ Tropical ○ Other_____

Weather Conditions _____

Color: ○ Black ○ Yellow ○ Brown ○ White ○ Blue ○ Red
○ Orange ○ Purple ○ Green ○ Striped ○ (Other) _____

Body: ○ Round/Chubby ○ Slender ○ Furry ○ (Other) _____

Stinger: ○ Yes ○ No

Behavior: ○ Solitary ○ Brood ○ Social ○ Parasitic ○ Aggressive
○ (Other) _____

Notes: _____

Wings
Head
Antennae
Thorax
Thorax
Foreleg
Middle Leg
Hindleg

Sketch

a. Similar to drone but have space between eyes.

b. Similar to worker but have shorter proboscis.

c. Have huge eyes that touch top of head.

a. **Worker** / b. **Queen** / c. **Drone**
○   ○   ○

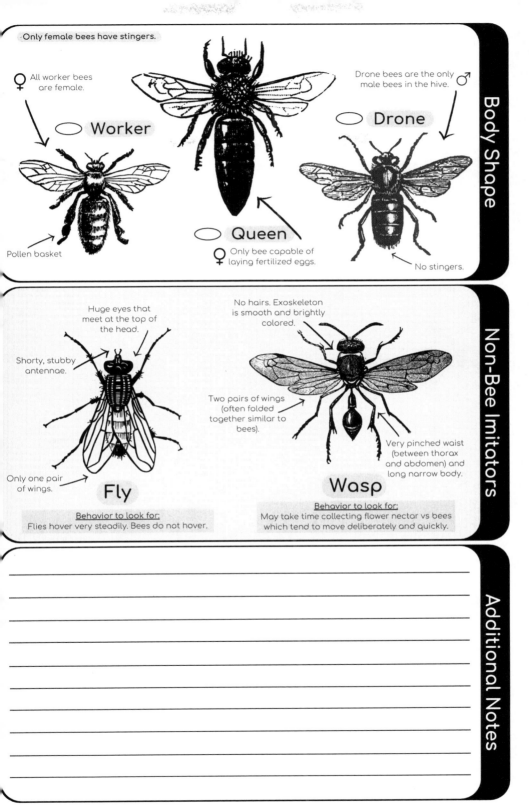

Only female bees have stingers.

♀ All worker bees are female.

◯ **Worker**

Drone bees are the only male bees in the hive. ♂

◯ **Drone**

Pollen basket

◯ **Queen**

♀ Only bee capable of laying fertilized eggs.

No stingers.

Huge eyes that meet at the top of the head.

Shorty, stubby antennae.

No hairs. Exoskeleton is smooth and brightly colored.

Two pairs of wings (often folded together similar to bees).

Only one pair of wings.

Fly

Very pinched waist (between thorax and abdomen) and long narrow body.

Wasp

Behavior to look for:
Flies hover very steadily. Bees do not hover.

Behavior to look for:
May take time collecting flower nectar vs bees which tend to move deliberately and quickly.

Location / GPS: _____ Date _____

Habitat: ◯ Garden ◯ Forest ◯ Woodland ◯ Orchard ◯ Meadow
◯ Other _____

Nest: ◯ Hive ◯ Wood ◯ Tree ◯ Hollow Stem/Reed ◯ Crevice/Edge
◯ Other _____

Climate Type: ◯ Dry ◯ Temperate ◯ Tropical ◯ Other_____

Weather Conditions _____

Color: ◯ Black ◯ Yellow ◯ Brown ◯ White ◯ Blue ◯ Red
◯ Orange ◯ Purple ◯ Green ◯ Striped ◯ (Other) _____

Body: ◯ Round/Chubby ◯ Slender ◯ Furry ◯ (Other) _____

Stinger: ◯ Yes ◯ No

Behavior: ◯ Solitary ◯ Brood ◯ Social ◯ Parasitic ◯ Aggressive
◯ (Other) _____

Notes: _____

Wings
Head
Antennae
Thorax
Thorax
Foreleg
Middle Leg
Hindleg

Sketch

a. Similar to drone but have space between eyes.

b. Similar to worker but have shorter proboscis.

c. Have huge eyes that touch top of head.

a. **Worker** / b. **Queen** / c. **Drone**
◯ ◯ ◯

Only female bees have stingers.

♀ All worker bees are female.

Drone bees are the only male bees in the hive. ♂

Worker

Drone

Pollen basket

Queen

♀ Only bee capable of laying fertilized eggs.

No stingers.

Huge eyes that meet at the top of the head.

No hairs. Exoskeleton is smooth and brightly colored.

Shorty, stubby antennae.

Two pairs of wings (often folded together similar to bees).

Very pinched waist (between thorax and abdomen) and long narrow body.

Only one pair of wings.

Fly

Wasp

Behavior to look for:
Flies hover very steadily. Bees do not hover.

Behavior to look for:
May take time collecting flower nectar vs bees which tend to move deliberately and quickly.

Environment

Location / GPS: _____ Date _____

Habitat: ○ Garden ○ Forest ○ Woodland ○ Orchard ○ Meadow
○ Other _____

Nest: ○ Hive ○ Wood ○ Tree ○ Hollow Stem/Reed ○ Crevice/Edge
○ Other _____

Climate Type: ○ Dry ○ Temperate ○ Tropical ○ Other _____

Weather Conditions _____

General

Color: ○ Black ○ Yellow ○ Brown ○ White ○ Blue ○ Red
○ Orange ○ Purple ○ Green ○ Striped ○ (Other) _____

Body: ○ Round/Chubby ○ Slender ○ Furry ○ (Other) _____

Stinger: ○ Yes ○ No

Behavior: ○ Solitary ○ Brood ○ Social ○ Parasitic ○ Aggressive
○ (Other) _____

Notes: _____

Characteristics

Wings →

Head

Antennae

Thorax

Thorax →

Foreleg

Middle Leg

Hindleg

Sketch

Head Shape

a.
Similar to drone but have space between eyes.

b.
Similar to worker but have shorter proboscis.

c.
Have huge eyes that touch top of head.

a. <u>Worker</u> / b. <u>Queen</u> / c. <u>Drone</u>
○   ○   ○

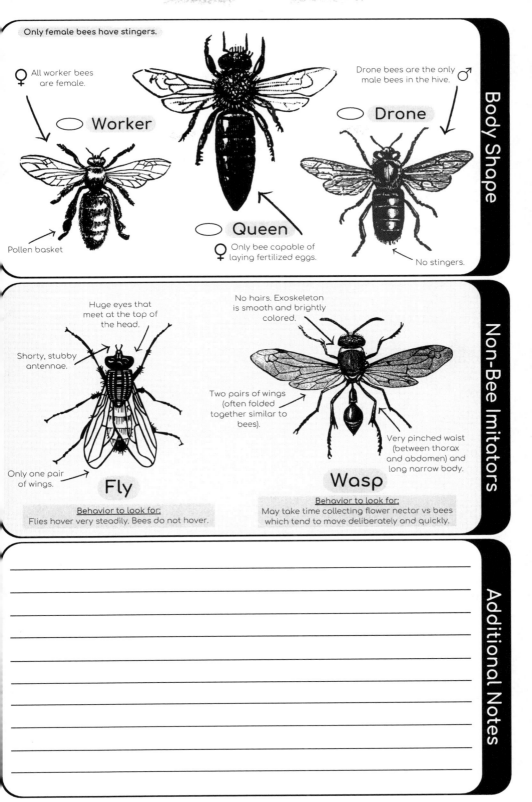

Only female bees have stingers.

♀ All worker bees are female.

⬭ Worker

Drone bees are the only male bees in the hive. ♂

⬭ Drone

Pollen basket

⬭ Queen

♀ Only bee capable of laying fertilized eggs.

No stingers.

Huge eyes that meet at the top of the head.

No hairs. Exoskeleton is smooth and brightly colored.

Shorty, stubby antennae.

Two pairs of wings (often folded together similar to bees).

Very pinched waist (between thorax and abdomen) and long narrow body.

Only one pair of wings. Fly

Wasp

Behavior to look for:
Flies hover very steadily. Bees do not hover.

Behavior to look for:
May take time collecting flower nectar vs bees which tend to move deliberately and quickly.

Environment

Location / GPS: _____ Date _____

Habitat: ◯ Garden ◯ Forest ◯ Woodland ◯ Orchard ◯ Meadow
◯ Other _____

Nest: ◯ Hive ◯ Wood ◯ Tree ◯ Hollow Stem/Reed ◯ Crevice/Edge
◯ Other _____

Climate Type: ◯ Dry ◯ Temperate ◯ Tropical ◯ Other_____

Weather Conditions _____

General

Color: ◯ Black ◯ Yellow ◯ Brown ◯ White ◯ Blue ◯ Red
◯ Orange ◯ Purple ◯ Green ◯ Striped ◯ (Other) _____

Body: ◯ Round/Chubby ◯ Slender ◯ Furry ◯ (Other) _____

Stinger: ◯ Yes ◯ No

Behavior: ◯ Solitary ◯ Brood ◯ Social ◯ Parasitic ◯ Aggressive
◯ (Other) _____

Notes: _____

Characteristics

Wings → Head
Antennae
Thorax
Thorax → Foreleg
Middle Leg
Hindleg

Sketch

Head Shape

a. Similar to drone but have space between eyes.

b. Similar to worker but have shorter proboscis.

c. Have huge eyes that touch top of head.

a. <u>Worker</u> / b. <u>Queen</u> / c. <u>Drone</u>
◯ ◯ ◯

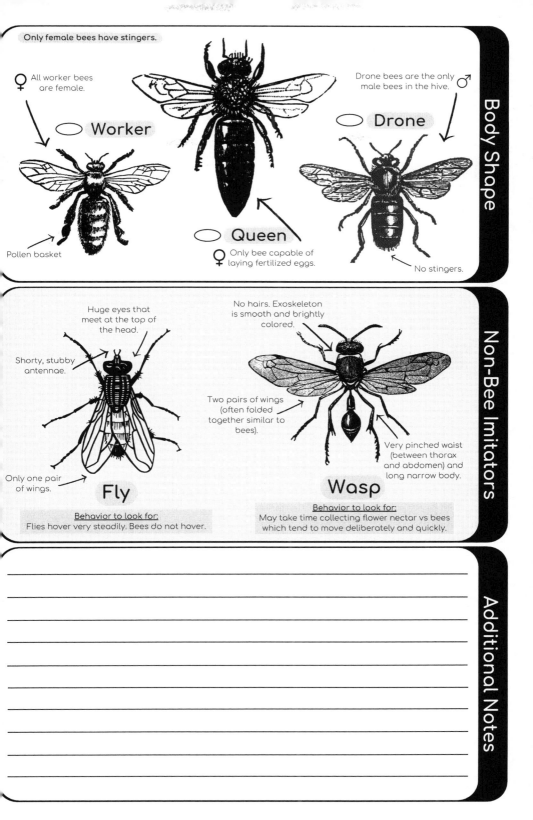

Only female bees have stingers.

♀ All worker bees are female.

Worker

Drone bees are the only male bees in the hive. ♂

Drone

Queen

Pollen basket

♀ Only bee capable of laying fertilized eggs.

No stingers.

Huge eyes that meet at the top of the head.

No hairs. Exoskeleton is smooth and brightly colored.

Shorty, stubby antennae.

Two pairs of wings (often folded together similar to bees).

Very pinched waist (between thorax and abdomen) and long narrow body.

Only one pair of wings.

Fly

Wasp

Behavior to look for:
Flies hover very steadily. Bees do not hover.

Behavior to look for:
May take time collecting flower nectar vs bees which tend to move deliberately and quickly.

Location / GPS: _____ **Date** _____

Habitat: ◯ Garden ◯ Forest ◯ Woodland ◯ Orchard ◯ Meadow
◯ Other _____

Nest: ◯ Hive ◯ Wood ◯ Tree ◯ Hollow Stem/Reed ◯ Crevice/Edge
◯ Other _____

Climate Type: ◯ Dry ◯ Temperate ◯ Tropical ◯ Other_____

Weather Conditions _____

Color: ◯ Black ◯ Yellow ◯ Brown ◯ White ◯ Blue ◯ Red
◯ Orange ◯ Purple ◯ Green ◯ Striped ◯ (Other) _____

Body: ◯ Round/Chubby ◯ Slender ◯ Furry ◯ (Other) _____

Stinger: ◯ Yes ◯ No

Behavior: ◯ Solitary ◯ Brood ◯ Social ◯ Parasitic ◯ Aggressive
◯ (Other) _____

Notes: _____

Wings
Head
Antennae
Thorax
Foreleg
Thorax
Middle Leg
Hindleg

Sketch

a.

Similar to drone but have space between eyes.

b.

Similar to worker but have shorter proboscis.

c.

Have huge eyes that touch top of head.

a. **Worker** / b. **Queen** / c. **Drone**
◯ ◯ ◯

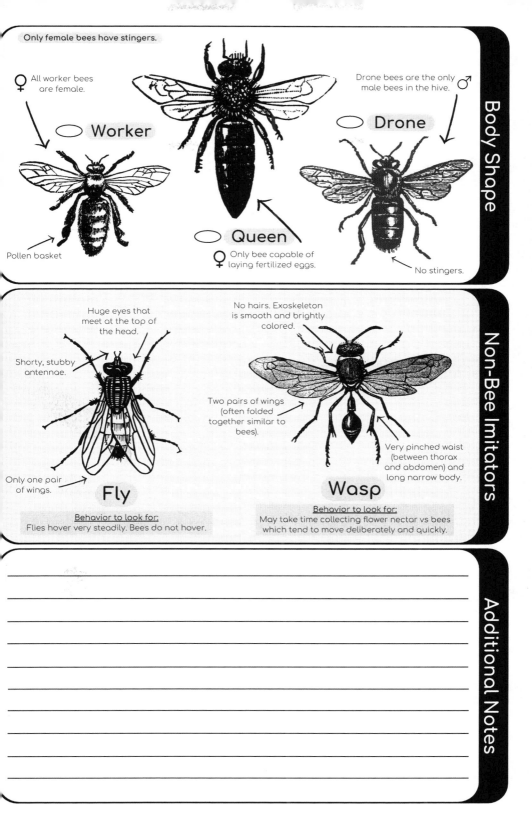

Only female bees have stingers.

All worker bees are female. ♀

○ **Worker**

Pollen basket

○ **Queen**
♀ Only bee capable of laying fertilized eggs.

Drone bees are the only male bees in the hive. ♂

○ **Drone**

No stingers.

Huge eyes that meet at the top of the head.

Shorty, stubby antennae.

Only one pair of wings.

Fly

Behavior to look for:
Flies hover very steadily. Bees do not hover.

No hairs. Exoskeleton is smooth and brightly colored.

Two pairs of wings (often folded together similar to bees).

Very pinched waist (between thorax and abdomen) and long narrow body.

Wasp

Behavior to look for:
May take time collecting flower nectar vs bees which tend to move deliberately and quickly.

Made in the USA
Monee, IL
17 May 2022